DESTINY'S HIGHWAY

DESTINY'S HIGHWAY

RIGHT IN FRONT OF YOUR FACE

MICHAEL G. QUIRK

Destiny's Highway: Right in Front of Your Face

Copyright © 2014 Michael G. Quirk

All rights reserved.

ISBN-10: 194114201X
ISBN-13: 978-1-941142-01-1

www.destinyshighway.com

I would like to dedicate this book to the part of me, the part of my soul that has been crucified and hammered to the point of absolute despair over many lifetimes. Without you experiencing and enduring these experiences/feelings I would not have felt what love is not and as a result I would not be able to understand and feel what love is today.

Thank you to my wife and family, and all the people, both past and present, who have supported me.

Right in Front of Our Face

Where is Peace?

Where is Truth?

Where is Calm?

Where is Purpose?

Where is it all, all that we want?

In a place where we would least expect.

In a place right in front of our face.

We struggle; we struggle every second of every minute of every day of our lives,

Trying to get to this place.

We are from there you know, a kind of hell, a place that makes us feel hopeless,

A place we were told not to go, or even contemplate.

So we look everywhere else, except a place where we all know, where we all can share no matter who we are from, royalty to the most humble of existences,

Because we were born there, a place we swore we would never, ever go back.

A fire, the start of it all, the beginning of the universe, the start of it all.

The beginnings of all beginnings.

This I'm afraid is how it all began,

So why am I struggling, why can't I get what I want?

So how can it be?

But it's a feeling every one of us knows, so it must be true, it is true, it is real.

So it did exist, and that's how it started and that's me and that's you and that's everyone and everything.

That's truth, that's calm, that's who we are.

So give me this feeling, I'll take it, I'll accept it. Now I know. I'll take this sword; I'll receive it gracefully.

The sword of where I was born, where we all began, a very humble place.

I can now accept it.

I now feel peace, but how can it be.

I now feel at one, like something I have never felt before.

It's uncanny; I now feel love for myself,

Now I can understand. I love who I am.

The struggle seems less; there's no judgment of anything or anyone.

It's wonderful, it's beautiful, and it's indescribable,

And it's been there all the time right in front of me, right in a place where I would least expect, right in front of my face.

It's all clear now, everything makes sense now,

How easy was that?

Too easy, no wonder I could never find it.

I was going to say thank you,

But it doesn't want thanking,

It's just happy that you now know,

And now it's over to you.

For your beginning

Love

Introduction

This book is a guide to help you find your answers. During the process, you'll feel the same as I did. There are times when you'll get it and half an hour later you won't. You'll get frustrated and annoyed, but then elated and peaceful. And then frustrated and annoyed and puzzled and ready for the next step. The feelings will fluctuate during the process of traveling, but try to always be gentle with yourself. There are different concepts outlined in different ways. You may get some but not others. You may get one explanation and not understand others, but if the message has been relayed clearly you may eventually understand the lot.

This book is about feelings, about changing your feelings to make yourself feel better without changing things in reality to do so. If you are not feeling well, nothing is worth anything.

I teach people that they can help themselves and get their own answers from a part of them that has always been trying to teach them. However, we're taught either it doesn't exist or not to listen to it and then indoctrinated to believe it's rubbish.

This book is part of a series. This first book in the series is a story about Fred Murray, his family, his friends, and his business associates. The story shows you a typical life of people who have learned to suppress their feelings and suffer consequences as a result. It also shows how you can break free and let go.

The second book in the series is an instructional book that gives more specific information about my techniques and how you can start yourself on the road to healing and happiness. Combined, these two books can help you change your life.

We were born to feel.

Chapter 1

"Hurry up and get ready for school, Brad. You'll miss the train. If you want me to drop you off at the train station, I'm leaving after I finish making your lunch in about ten minutes."

Rosa felt it was her motherly duty to get her two teenagers moving in the morning.

"What's he doing? Can you go and see what in the hell your brother is up to, Deb?"

"Mom, he's not out of bed, yet," Deb yelled.

"What? By the living...."

She stormed into her son's bedroom and saw him under the covers. "I've had enough of this. You can't hide away from the world every time you don't want to do something. Now get up or you can forget about going to the beach this weekend."

Brad groaned. "Ah, but mom, I hate school. I don't want to go."

Having dealt with this sort of behavior all his life, Rosa was thanking her lucky stars there was only one more year of schooling left for him. But what would happen then? That was an even scarier thought.

"I'm not interested at all in your whining. All I want is to see you in the kitchen dressed for school in five minutes, young man, otherwise there'll be hell to pay." She walked back to the kitchen.

Damn it, we haven't got any fresh bread for their lunches, Rosa said to herself. She looked around until she spied an older loaf at the back of the cupboard. *It's a bit old, but what the heck,* she thought.

"Mom, you can't use that bread. It's got mold on it," Deb said.

"Well, you'll have to buy your lunch, then. I'll give you some money. Where's my purse? Can you look for it while I chase your brother up?"

"What are you doing, Brad?" yelled Rosa again.

"I'm on the toilet, Mom!"

"Well hurry up!" Rosa was getting more upset by the second.

"Mom, there's a certain thing you can't hurry up," Brad said, in an attempt to lighten his mother up.

"I don't care; we should have left by now." Rosa was almost resigned to running late again.

"Mom, I can't find your purse," Deb yelled from the hallway.

"Have you looked in the car?" asked Rosa.

"No, I haven't."

"Well that would be good!" Rosa's patience had run out.

"Okay, no need to be so snappy," Deb said.

"Don't give me that attitude, young lady, just go and look in the car."

While trying to clean her teeth Rosa discovered she was out of toothpaste. *Damn. Out of toothpaste. I'll have to remember to get some.*

"Mom, your bag is in the car but the car is locked. Where are the car keys?"

No, no, no, I don't believe this—why does this keep on happening? Rosa thought. I'm going to be late again. I've been late for work more times than I can remember. Something always goes wrong. I was going to get a spare key cut, but I haven't got around to it. I keep forgetting.

"Mom, do you know where my basketball shirt is? We've

got a game on this arvo," yelled Brad, "Remember? I told you last week."

"When? No you didn't."

"Yes I did, when you were in the kitchen talking to dad about how you had to put the new microwave in to be fixed. They called to say it was ready to be picked up and Dad asked, 'Is that the store near the basketball stadium?' and you said, 'Yes,' and I said, 'I have a game today,' and you said that you could take me after work and pick the microwave up at the same time, remember?"

She didn't remember, but she wasn't going to let him know. The best thing to do now that he had her on the defense was to attack. Every mom knew that.

"Yes, that's right. Haven't I told you to get your gear ready the night before? How old are you? Seventeen. And how many times have I told to get you gear ready the night before? So don't whine to me about it, that's your problem."

You have to be kidding me, she thought. *As if I don't have enough problems of my own, like the case of the missing car keys.*

"I'm off to school, Mom. Don't worry about lunch, I'll get some from someone or I'll go without. See you." Deb walked up the street to where her friend Lyn lived and traveled with her to school.

"Bye, have a nice day," Rosa's replied as Deb left the usual chaos behind.

Now what have I done with those keys? Rosa thought.

"Okay, Mom, I'm ready," Brad proudly proclaimed. "I found my basketball shirt, it was in the laundry. It's unwashed and stinks a bit, but it'll be all right. They won't be watching me too closely today—my odor will protect me," Brad joked. But he was talking to himself because his mom had gone into the bedroom to finish getting ready.

As Rosa was putting her make-up on, she called her husband, Fred, from the bedroom phone.

"Mr. Murray. Your wife is on line two," his receptionist, Pam, called out and then softly to everyone else whispered, "yet again."

"Please excuse me, gentleman," Fred said. He was in the middle of a conference and wasn't thrilled to take the phone call.

"Hello, what is it now?" Fred Murray felt he was a busy man with an image to protect. It didn't look good having a wife calling him up so many times—always with a problem.

"Do you know where my car keys are?" Rosa pleaded.

"What time is it? Good God, woman, you should have left by now. You're late for work again."

"Yes, yes, but where are they?"

"Maybe they're on the chair down the side in the lounge room where you fell asleep last night." Fred could tell Rosa was panicky. "Now don't get flustered, calm down and take deep breaths. Remember what the therapist said? How is that new medication going, anyhow?"

"No different than the last one."

"Don't forget to take it three times a day. Okay, now go and have a look in the lounge and I'll stay on the phone," instructed Fred.

Rosa looked and reported back. "No, not there. I feel so stupid. I can't cope anymore." She started to lose her composure.

"Now come on, where's my good girl? You'll be fine, everyone makes mistakes. You'll be late again, better call your work up and just tell them. Look, I've got to go now, my people are waiting for me, you'll be fine. Bye." Fred was about to sign off from a conversation he'd had too often. He paused for a moment to pop a pill to help his stomach ulcer before he returned to the conference room to continue his performance. Rosa squeezed in one last request.

"Can you get Brad to basketball today? I'm going to have to work back." She pushed her luck even further and added, "Can you pick up the microwave as well?"

"I'll see what I can do. Now go!"

"Bye." With a tear in her eye, Rosa took a moment to pull herself together.

Just then Brad walked in, saw his mom upset and gave

her a hug. "What's up, Mom? What's he done now?" *It's usually Dad*, Brad thought.

"No, no nothing. I can't find my car keys."

Brad's started to explain in a sheepish tone, "Last night I decided to start practicing at reversing the car because I'll be starting to learn how to drive, and I put your keys in my pocket." He reached in and pulled them out. "And I still have them. Here they are. Sorry, Mom," he said as he handed over the keys.

Happy to have the problem solved, all Rosa could say was, "Come on, Brad, let's go. In the car."

On the driveway, Brad said, "Here's a note from my teachers, they want to meet with you." Brad retrieved a scrunched up note from his school bag, flattened it out, and gave it to Rosa.

> *Dear Mr. and Mrs. Murray,*
>
> *We wish to meet with you to discuss Brad's*
>
> ** Lack of application to his studies,*
>
> ** Failure to do homework, and*
>
> ** Complete his tasks in the classroom.*
>
> *Head Teacher*

It was too much for Rosa to cope with, too much for her to handle, and it was only the beginning of the day. *It's going to be one of those days*, she thought. These sorts of days were becoming more and more frequent.

"Brad, I don't want to know about it right now, we'll talk about it tonight." She stashed the scrunched up letter in the glove box.

Rosa dropped Brad off at the train station, but the trains were held up. There were signs telling the commuters of a problem with the line. The sign said that they didn't know when it was going to be fixed, but that buses would transport the passengers.

"Oh dear, what a shame. I guess I'll have to miss out on school," chirped Brad

"No way—we pay a lot of money for you to go to that school and you can't afford to miss any more time. You can wait until the buses come to take you."

"Okay. What about my lunch?"

"Here," she said giving Brad a twenty-dollar note. "That's all I have."

"Cool."

"I want some change."

"Sure, sure. Bye!"

Chapter 2

As Rosa walked in the office door, the receptionist asked, "What's the story today, Rosa? Car trouble, kid trouble, husband trouble? Mr. Johnson wanted to see you when you arrived."

What now? Rosa thought as she walked into his office.

"Sit down, Rosa. Now as long as I've been the boss here, I've never come across someone that comes in late as often as you do. If it were anyone else, I would've got rid of them a long time ago, but you're an excellent worker. You're very thorough and you can solve the hard cases no one else can. I don't want to let you go, but the other workers think I'm favoring you. That's why I'm going to create another position for you allowing you to work more flexible hours. That way, if you come in late, you can finish later. As long as the work is done. You'll be Assistant Supervisor. Your pay will remain the same, but you'll be part of management, so you'll have to attend the manager's meeting on Tuesday mornings. I'm sure you'll be happier with that. I know you're on medication, so let's hope this arrangement will make everything less stressful for you."

"Thank you, Mr. Johnson. I'll do my best."

"I know. You always do, Rosa."

Michael G. Quirk

* * *

At morning teatime, Fred briefly wondered how late Rosa was going to arrive at work this time. Her weakness made him look bad and he wondered how many people looked at him as a failure, not only in business, but in relationships as well. At least he had Pam and she respected him. He knew he couldn't leave Rosa to be with Pam, but it sure felt good to have at least one person in his life that looked up to him and accepted him as he was.

Fred's business wasn't going so well. He thought about the latest figures coming in on sales for the month. They weren't good, and as the main owner of the business, they reflected on him. It was time to bring in the salesmen and motivate them to achieve their goals. He needed to make them work as hard as he did.

Having attended many seminars on motivation, public speaking, and promotion, he spent some time pumping himself up and bringing back that old spark that had helped him when he started the company with the help of his friend, Barry Heaton. He would have to call on all his resources to inspire the team once again and make them do what they needed to do for the company.

After gathering his thoughts together and preparing his speech, he brought his sales team together and delivered his usual speech with great gusto. It may have sounded trite and repetitive, but he believed every word he said. In fact, he wished his wife and son would take a page out of his book. Like him, anyone could achieve success by being the best that they could be and having a positive mental attitude. Once again, he saved the team and he could see the salesmen were inspired to go out and conquer the world.

"Mr. Murray. There's a problem," his sales manager, Schofields, said as he entered the room.

"What's that? Come on in and let's talk about it." Fred settled at his desk.

Schofields cleared his throat. "Even if our sales figures are adjusted on a seasonal basis, our figures have never been so low. Some of the sales team are telling us that there's new opposition from overseas that has entered the market with a better product than ours and they've won some of our clients."

Stunned by the news, the thoughts of Fred's previous business failures again resurfaced. Fred didn't know what to say at first, but being a survivor, he thanked Schofields for the information, put on his brave face, and immediately called his partner, Barry.

Barry was a well-established businessman who had many different businesses all over the world. To him, helping this business get off its feet was just a favor to his old college mate. He knew Fred's history in business, but was prepared to contribute 25% to help Fred in this venture. After all, if Fred was prepared to mortgage his house, it was on Fred's back if he didn't make it work. He didn't care if the business failed; it was no skin off his teeth. Also, Barry had insisted that his 25% was his one and only injection of funds and there would not be any more from him. Fred would have to live or die on his own efforts.

However, as unlucky as Fred was in business matters, Barry had the same bad luck with women in relationships. He had lost count of how many live-in partners he'd had. He concentrated on the thing he was good at and that was making money.

When Fred called, Barry was going through another crisis of his own. His latest girlfriend had just thrown another tantrum. She wrecked his place and punched him repeatedly. To defend himself, he restrained her and held her to the ground so she wouldn't cause further damage. After she calmed down, she called the police and told them that Barry assaulted her and violated her. Believing her, they took Barry down to the police station.

Fred knew that Barry had enough of his own problems

and didn't know what to say anyway—after all, he was no expert on relationships. He wasn't able to talk to Barry about the business and all Barry had said in that respect was that he couldn't invest any more money. Fred couldn't help Barry with his relationship problems, either, so he ended the phone call with a bad feeling in his gut. He knew his business was barely holding on and if he made the wrong move, it would all come crashing down around him.

That afternoon, Fred spent time with Schofields trying to work out strategies to boost their sales. No matter what they came up with, it meant spending more money, and Fred didn't have any more to spend, and Barry had already made his position clear. He saw no option but to let people go, but if that happened, then people would know that Fred was a failure once again. His solution was to get some of his staff to leave on their own. That way he would still look like the good guy and the staff would look like losers for leaving when times got hard. He was good at manipulating people to work harder, so why not manipulate them to quit?

He told Schofields to come up with ways to get some people to leave on their own and he would do the same.

"Yes, sir, Mr. Murray, whatever you think. You're the boss." As he walked back to his office, Schofields thought that his boss was losing his marbles and thought it wise to look for another job. He could see that it was the beginning of the end for the business.

Back in his office, Schofields called Barry Heaton. "Hello, Mr. Heaton," Schofields said. You told me to keep an eye on things and I think you'll want to hear the latest."

"What's he up to now?" Barry asked.

"I tell you, he's lost his marbles. He's facing a minor crisis because of some competition from overseas. All he has to do is keep his main sales going, downsize, and concentrate on his share of the market. But he doesn't want to look like the bad guy and let people go, so he's trying to come up with these crazy plans to get staff to leave on their own. What's worse, earlier today he gave them all a big pep talk. To add to his delusions of grandeur, he thinks he's a great motivational speaker and that all he had to do is talk and people will do whatever he asks."

"You're right, he's off his rocker. But business is business, Schofields; it's time for you to leave. I have an opening in your hometown—a management position at your old job. The present guy is going to be gotten rid of due to family problems. You can start next week if you like."

"Sounds good to me, I'll be there. Thanks for looking out for me."

"Not at all, Schofields. You're a good man."

At 4:00 p.m., Fred was interrupted by Schofields. "I have some bad news Mr. Murray. I just got a call from my hometown hospital to say that my mother has taken a bad turn and I should come home and see her, so I'm heading there right now. I'll call and tell you what's happening when I get there."

"Of course, Schofields, of course. Go ahead and get down there." *Great, now who's going to set the plots to force the salesmen to go?* he thought. He continued to work on his plans, completely forgetting Brad's basketball game and that he was supposed to pick him up afterward. He opened a desk drawer and pulled out a bottle.

Chapter 3

Brad's basketball team was not the best. Their team was not above average in skill, but the boys enjoyed each other's company and they had fun. They didn't really have a coach—nobody could be bothered. If any parents came at all to watch the game, they usually just tried to encourage them. But the boys preferred and were old enough to organize themselves. Besides, they didn't take to being told how to play better. They just wanted to do their own thing.

Brad was dismayed when his mother messaged to inform him that his father would be at his game later that day. From past experience, Brad knew his father wouldn't just come and watch the game like other parents. No, he would try and coach them as if they played for the NBA. It was very embarrassing. He'd shout out standard calls that he had heard on television, try and get all the players in a huddle to scream "go team," or other such motivational cheers, and then he'd talk a lot of stuff that the boys knew was a lot of crap.

When the game was over, Brad would get told on the way home what he should've been doing better and what he did wrong and how he should be ashamed of the way he played and wasn't he embarrassed to walk onto the court? And had he ever won a game? His father would ask him why he didn't practice. That if he never studied, then he would never be a success, and if he didn't pass his next exam, he would be a nobody. About how he wouldn't be going to the beach and on and on and on. Brad could hear it going on in his head throughout the day.

So the thought of his father coming to his game put a damper, not only on his playtime, but also on the rest of his day, and his game of fun turned from something enjoyable into something that he had to do to please someone else.

As the boys ran onto the court, Brad was relieved to see that his father was not there. At halftime, his father was still not there and Brad began to wonder who was going to pick him up. At the end of the game, Brad was left alone as he waved good-bye to his friends. He messaged his mom who was still at work, "hey mom whats happening? finished game, where's dad?"

Rosa was away from her desk when her mobile buzzed. She was trying to catch up on her day at work. As a result, she didn't hear the message come through. After ten minutes of watching the next game of basketball, Brad figured that his mom hadn't got the message and he wanted to stay away from Dad so he decided to ring Rosa's dad—good old Pop.

Pop was now retired from his work; in fact, he had retired five times. He achieved financial success over and over again. He did exceedingly well for an immigrant arriving in the country with nothing more than a suitcase. He spent his time playing the stock market and going fishing. Both Grandma and Grandpa had not taken well to being idle. They both involved themselves in the lives of their daughters and their families. In their opinion, both their daughters had not grown up yet, and they would always need their help.

Coming to Brad's rescue was fine with his grandpa. This would be more proof in his eyes that Rosa married a no-hoper. In his day, the mother's job was to be at home with the children and it was the husband's job to provide for his family. If Fred wasn't so hopeless, Rosa would be there for her son.

Brad was a street-smart kid; he could see the dynamics

and could play things to his advantage. He had his grandparents' phone number in his mobile for such occasions. It was not the first or last time that Brad and his sister Deb had been left in the lurch.

He held down "G" which started the quick-dial. It rang.

"Hello, Pop."

"Yes, hello."

"It's Brad, Pop. How are you doing? What are you up to?"

"Oh, Brad, yes, I'm just doing some gardening, getting some tomatoes out of the garden. How about you?"

"I'm at the basketball stadium. Just finished my game. Dad was supposed to be picking me up but he hasn't shown. I can't get hold of Mom; I sent her a message but haven't heard from her. So I was wondering—"

"Say no more, Brad. I'll be there in fifteen minutes."

"Oh, don't worry, Pop, I'll get a lift home off someone. I was just wondering if you were going to a soccer game this weekend. That last game you took me to was great!"

"How are you getting home? That's not right. It's no trouble Brad, I'll be there in fifteen minutes."

"Are you sure, Pop? I don't want to put you out."

"No trouble at all."

"Thanks, Pop!"

As promised, Pop was there to pick Brad up in fifteen minutes.

"Is there anyone at home, now?" asked Pop.

"Maybe Deb is," replied Brad.

"Can you give her a call to see if she's on her own?"

Deb was in her room studying hard for an upcoming exam and was looking forward to the trip overseas that she won as an ambassador for her region of World Friends and Companions later in the year. Deb had never been any trouble and always did the right thing. She was intelligent and seemed far more mature than her fifteen years of age.

Deb picked up the phone and heard Brad's voice. "Hey, dopey. Is anyone home with you?"

"What's it to you, dero?" she replied.

"I'm with Pop in his car, he wants to know if you've heard from Mom or Dad."

"No. Mom will be working late because she was late this morning. I guess Dad will be home whenever."

"Hang on, I'll tell Pop." Brad spoke to Pop and returned to the conversation with his sister.

"Pop wants to know if you and I want to go over to their place for dinner."

"Tell Pop thanks, but I have too much homework to do and I'll be fine."

"Suit yourself. I'm going to Pop's place. Can you tell them whenever they get home?"

"Shall do. See ya!"

"Yeah, see ya dopey."

After a few more minutes of driving, Pop pulled into his driveway and Brad was greeted by Nan. "Hello, Bradley my boy. My, you are getting tall. Come and give Nan a hug."

"Hi, Nan."

Once they got inside she asked, "Would you like some of my orange cake?"

"Great, thanks," Brad said as he took two pieces.

"How did your basketball game go?"

"Oh, we lost again, but it was fun."

"Do you want to help us pick tomatoes from the garden? I'm going to make some relish."

"Sure thing, Nan; your tomato relish is mighty fine, if I do say so myself."

"Thanks, Brad. Let's go, we need about twenty pounds—here's a bucket."

"Nan, I'd better let Mom know where I am. I'll send her another message."

Just as Rosa was about to leave for the day, she heard her mobile beep. She saw that she had two unread messages.

From Brad, "*at nan and pops. dad no show. pop picked me up.*"

And then, *"hey mom whats happening? finished game, where's dad?"*

Rosa was mad at Fred for forgetting to pick up Brad and at the thought of going to her parents place to face the usual from her father about Fred.

Rosa pushed the "P" on her mobile and waited for them to answer.

"Mom?"

"Rosalind?"

"I'm sorry that Brad rang you. Thanks for picking him up."

"That's no trouble, dear. He's in the backyard picking tomatoes."

"I'll come and get him. I'll be there in half an hour."

"There is no rush, Rosalind. He was going to stay for dinner."

"No, he's fine, Mom. I'll come and get him. Bye, Mom."

She said Rosalind, Rosa thought, *I'm in for it now. She had heard it all before. "What sort of mother would leave her children at the basketball stadium? You should be at home with the children. You shouldn't have married that no-hoper. We warned you he was no good. He's never there and he doesn't provide for you."* She heard their voices already.

As Rosa drove over to her parents' place to pick up her son, she began to cry. She had been diagnosed with depression three years before, and she felt that it had come back again even with her medication. The way she felt after the day she was having, she contemplated briefly about driving her car into a tree. She had had enough. But by the time she had arrived at her parents' place, she had managed to pull herself together once again to face the music.

"Hello, Dad."

Her father just gave her a glance that said, "Wake up to yourself" and kept walking.

"Hi, Mom," said Brad.

"Let's go, Brad." Rosa ordered.

"You know, your father and I love you, and we're here to support you in any way, Rosalind."

"Yes, I know, Mom, thanks again."

"How's new microwave we gave you working out?"

"Oh, it's fine. It's a great help when we get home from work late and get dinner quickly."

"If you need anything, just let us know."

Rosa turned away so her mother wouldn't see the tear in her eye.

"Thanks again, Mom."

The way home was silent until Brad spoke. "I like being over there. You must've had a great childhood with them. They're so nice."

"You think so?"

"What's the deal with the microwave? Why didn't you tell them it was broken?"

"It's not worth the trouble, trust me. That reminds me, that microwave still needs to be picked up. Great, what am I going to cook for tea without the microwave?"

When they arrived home, they found Fred out on the back patio having a drink or three and smoking his smelly cigars. Already over the limit, he blurted out, "Where have you been?"

"Picking your son up!" Rosa fired back.

"Things are not good at work and I forgot all about it." As he opened the fridge for another beer, he turned his attention to Brad. "Anyway, how'd you do, boy? Lose again?"

Jerk, Brad thought, but didn't say anything.

Rosa was speechless as she came through the kitchen door with groceries in hand. "What's for dinner, Mom?" asked Brad.

"I don't know, son. I have no microwave." She stared at Fred.

"What? Don't blame me. I've got problems at work."

Trying to be nice so his mom didn't remember about the note from school and to stop the usual verbal battle between his parents, Brad offered to help get dinner ready.

"What do you want? Money? How much and what for?" Rosa asked and smiled.

"I don't want money. Just thought I'd help," Brad replied.

Fred called out at Rosa. "Have you fed the dog yet, woman? He keeps looking up at me."

"No, he wants to go for a walk, Dad." Deb came out with her aerobics gear on. "I'm taking him for a walk."

"Why didn't you pick up Brad and the microwave?" asked Rosa.

"I never said I would—I said I'd see what I could do. Besides, it's not my job. I've got more important things to do than go to some lame basketball game and pick up your parents' microwave. We don't need their charity, anyway."

Oh no, here we go again, thought Brad. He knew the telltale tone of voice his dad used before he went off. "I'll peel the potatoes, Mom. We can boil them on the stove."

"It's not my job to run errands," Fred said. "My job is to provide for this family. I'm—I'm fully occupied at work." Fred began to stumble over his words. "I work hard and long for the good of this family, and all I get is disrespect, and I'm not appreciated." He grabbed another drink from the fridge. He lost count of how many he'd had and figured it didn't matter anyway. He was the boss; he could do what he liked both at home and at work.

"So you expect me to go back there tomorrow and pick the microwave up because you forgot it? You just think I'm a maid—you have no respect for me. I'm here just at your beck and call," Rosa said.

Sweet, Brad thought, *I'm off the hook. Mom and Dad are going at it again; I'm free for the night.* He had only seen it hundreds of times. As it usually happened, Dad out-argued Mom, thought he won, went off to the pub, and came home drunk and had to sleep in the other room because Mom had locked him out of the bedroom. Mom went to bed early, took her sleeping pills to fall asleep, and Brad could do whatever he wanted. Deb was too goody-good to do anything wrong, and as her dad and mom said, "She never gives us any trouble." Everything was right on cue.

"Don't worry about dinner for me; your cooking is garbage, anyway. I'm off to the pub."

"You can't drive. You've been drinking too much."

"Shut it, woman," he said as went out the back door.

"I hate him, Mom; he's a jerk," Brad said.

She was so used to it; she worked on autopilot as she continued to cook dinner.

Deb came out of her room, had dinner and went back to her room. Nobody said anything. "Can you clean up please, son? I'm going to bed."

"Sure, Mom." He gave her a kiss good night.

Rosa made it to her bathroom and then collapsed in a ball on the floor of the shower. Eventually, she managed to get up, dry herself off, and get dressed.

She brushed her teeth without toothpaste—she forgot to buy some when she went grocery shopping. "I'm so hopeless," she said to herself as she looked in the mirror. "Maybe I should just end it now." She opened the drawer where she kept her pills.

Chapter 4

The next morning Deb woke up first. She found her dad hung over on the recliner. Mom had taken too many sleeping pills and was going to be late again. Brad was still in bed. She turned on the radio, hoping that the noise it made would get things going. She didn't worry about breakfast. She didn't want to put on weight; she had to be thin.

She couldn't be bothered with her family and took herself off to her friend Lyn's place.

"Hello, Deb. You're early this morning."

"Hello, Mrs. Booker. Is Lyn ready for school, yet?"

"She's in her room. She's not feeling that well today, coming down with a virus, I think. I don't think she's going today. You can go in and see her if you like."

As Deb knocked on the door she called out, "Lyn? It's Deb. Can I come in?"

"Yeah, sure."

"How are you feeling?"

"Oh, I've got this headache and I feel sick in the stomach."

"But you can't miss out today, we have our exams. They count towards our final grade. Why don't you take something for it and come to school?"

"No, no I can't, it's too bad. I'll have to miss out."

"You get this a lot, don't you? You poor thing."

"I'll tell the teacher that I saw you and tell them you won't be coming."

"Thanks."

"Gee, you're lucky. I wouldn't be allowed to stay home if I were sick, my parents would just send me on my way no matter how sick I was," Deb said.

"Mom is okay, but Dad just thinks I'm faking it. Mom and Dad fight about it all the time.

Do you know what you're going to do next year? What subjects you're going do to, what career path you are going to take?" asked Lyn.

"Yes, I want to do teaching, but Dad wants me to do accounting and Mom wants me to do physiotherapy," Deb said. She began to chew her nails.

"I don't have a clue. I know Mom and Dad have spent a lot of money on my education, but I don't know what I want to do with it." Lyn chewed her nails in unison with Deb.

"You better hurry up because we have to have our choices in by next week."

"Yep, I know," Lyn sighed.

"Anyway, I better go and catch the bus. I'll see you tomorrow." Deb got up from the side of the bed.

"Bye, Deb, good luck in the exam today."

"Thanks."

Deb said goodbye to Lyn's mom on the way out.

"See you later, Mrs. Booker."

"Deb, do you know if your mother is playing basketball with us tonight?"

"I don't know. She probably has to work late again," Deb answered.

"We play the late game, so she should be all right, don't you think?"

"Yeah, I guess. Why don't you give her a call at work? I'll see you later."

* * *

Rosa woke up, late again, and tried to remember what happened the night before. It came back to her as she showered. She had taken a couple of extra sleeping meds, and when they started to kick in, she somehow dragged herself to bed and passed out. Every day it seemed to get a little harder to wake up. *Maybe I need different meds.*

She dropped Brad off at school and made it to work only an hour later than normal. Thank goodness for her new schedule.

* * *

After leaving Lyn's house, Deb walked down to the bus stop and waited for the bus that took her to school. Lost in her thoughts, she didn't notice the man sitting at the bus stop until she almost sat on him. Embarrassed, she turned red and apologized and then sat down on the far side of the bench.

Glancing over at him, she saw he was rough looking, but seemed kind. He looked up at her and smiled and then went back to reading his book. When the bus pulled up, he got on behind Deb and sat in the seat next to her. She smiled shyly and said hello and then looked out the window.

* * *

After Deb left, Lyn's mom came into the room. "I'll be going to the gym shortly. Is there anything I can get for you while I'm out?"

"No thanks, Mom."

Sarah gave her a daughter a kiss on the forehead and left the room.

Sarah Booker loved her time at the gym—not only for the exercise but for the interaction with the other women.

"Who is that? Is that you, Sally? You look great. Where have you been? The last time I saw you, now let's think, you were having your third visit to the hospital. That must have been about three years ago."

"Hey, Sarah. Yes, that's about right. This is my first day

back at the gym. I thought I'd get back and do a bit today."

"How did it all go? They must have done you good?"

"The depression returned again soon after I left the hospital for the second time. Because I felt that I had exhausted all the options available I thought that I was beyond help. I was in despair. My friend got sick of me wanting to kill myself and sat down with me and looked at alternatives. Anyway, to make a long story short, I went to this guy named Michael who taught me lots of different things, but mainly how to love myself and that my health and happiness are in my hands. He showed me how to do it. It really worked for me and so here I am."

"That's terrific! What medication have they got you on now?"

"I'm not on any."

"That's amazing. Your hair is different, you look different, you are glowing, that's all I can say, Sally."

"How's your family?" asked Sally.

"Fine, fine. James is working hard, and Lyn, well—"

"How old is she now?" Sally interrupted.

"Fifteen."

"Really? Wow, time flies. I can still remember when you used to come around and the two little ones used to play. My John and your Lyn down at the beach."

"Yes, poor Lyn isn't going too well at the moment. She's at home today. She gets sick all the time."

"Really?"

"Yeah. Don't really know what it is, but I'm getting a bit tired of the hassle. James can't stand her being sick. He says she's faking it and that she just wants to get out of school. She needs help of some sort, but I don't know what to do."

"Listen, I'll give you Michael's number and you can call and ask him. He might be able to steer you in the right direction."

"That would be great. Let's go in; the class is about to start."

Upon returning home, Sarah called Michael's number.

"Hello, Michael Quirk speaking," came the answer.

"Hello. My name is Sarah and I was given your name by Sally Ryan who has been to see you."

"Yes, Sally, I remember her."

"You see, I don't know if you can help me, but can I ask you about my daughter?"

"Sure, go ahead. How old is she?"

"She's fifteen and she gets sick all the time, mainly when she's going to school and when exams or competitions are on. She's physically sick—she does vomit and she gets headaches. She's really talented. She can sing really well on her own or with the family, but she can't do it in front of an audience. She's at home in bed now. What can I do to help her? Can you help her?"

"That depends on her. Does she want to be helped? Does she think it's a problem?"

"Well, I don't know. I think she does. She doesn't know that I'm talking to you."

"Well, you see, what I do is help people learn about themselves on a feeling level. Basically I help them learn what love is by loving themselves and that their health and happiness are in their hands. To do that, there needs to be a part of her that chooses to do that. If that part is there, then we can help it. So have a talk to her about wanting to feel better about herself and about learning how to feel stronger and more confident. It's learning how your feelings work for you. It's not therapy, it's just learning."

"Okay, then, I'll talk to her."

"If she does decide to come, call back and make an appointment."

"Thank you."

As the day went on, Lyn realized that she was at the stage where she was sick of being sick. By the time Sarah returned, she was looking for some relief. When Sarah came in and suggested that she go and have a talk to someone, Lyn agreed.

"Michael said it was just learning about yourself, and you should have seen Sally—she was glowing."

"Sally who?" asked Lyn.

"Remember the lady whose backyard near the beach you used to play in when you were younger?"

"You mean Mrs. Ryan?"

"Yes that's her."

"Didn't she go crazy or something?"

"No, no. She was suffering from depression and she had to spend some time in the hospital, that's all."

"But I remember Dad saying she was a nutter and that's why we didn't go over there anymore."

"Don't listen to your father; she's really good. Anyhow, I'll ring up and make an appointment."

After she called Michael and made an appointment, she informed Lyn.

"I rang up, Lyn. You're going to see Michael next Thursday after school at four p.m."

"Okay, Mom." Lyn got a feeling of dread in the pit of her stomach. *What's he going to think of me? Will he say that I'm crazy and need to be put away somewhere? I don't like people trying to figure me out.*

Chapter 5

Brad was the first one to arrive home and was happy to be alone because he could practice his guitar that his friend had lent him. Despite the opposition of his father, Brad still wanted a guitar, but his father wouldn't be in it. He said it was a waste of money. He would use it for a week and that would be that. However, his friend had an old one and lent it to him.

He was taking music at school. In fact, he was a natural. But in his father's world, it was a waste of time. Not only could Brad play quite well, he could also sing. When he was on his own, he could let himself go and try and play some of his original compositions that he made up while taking retreat in his room, away from the parental squabbles that frequently occurred.

He played his piece over and over again, making adjustments until he felt it was right. On his final run he didn't hear his sister come through the door.

What is that noise? Deb thought. *Did they leave the radio on this morning?* It was coming from Brad's room. Was that Brad playing? She stopped and listened. He was good, very good. At the end of the piece she stuck her head around the corner into his room.

"Brad, that was really good. I didn't know you could play

so well and sing so well. And who wrote that song?"

"Thanks, dopey, I did."

He was feeling quite happy with himself. "I'm going to be playing at the end of the year on presentation night—a solo. I've been chosen. Only two people have been chosen and I'm one," Brad informed his sister.

"Do Mom and Dad know?" asked Deb.

"No, I'm not telling them. It is a surprise, so don't you tell them, dopey!"

"Don't worry, I won't. It will be a surprise, all right!"

Just then the phone rang. "Hello, Murray residence," Deb answered. It was her mom.

"Hello, Deb. I'm ringing to tell you that I'm going straight to basketball. I'll be home after that. Are you and your brother okay?"

"Yes, we're fine. When is Dad coming home?"

"I don't know," came a voice that sounded like it couldn't care less about the answer to that question.

"Okay, see you."

"Mom is playing basketball until late tonight, and I don't know where Dad is. So why don't you keep practicing, and I'll stay and look out for you." Deb wanted to listen to some more of Brad's playing.

"Thanks."

"Do you mind if I stay and listen to you?"

"No, you just have to pay me, that's all."

"I'm going to call Dad up and see what he's doing." Deb reached for the phone and dialed. "That's funny. No one is answering the phone in his office. I'll try his mobile. It just goes to voice mail. She left a message. "Dad, its Deb, can you bring home some take out dinner for us? Mom is playing basketball 'til late. Thanks."

"Go for it, Bradley," Deb said. "Ladies and gentlemen, I want you to make some noise and welcome to the stage—Bradley Murray." Clapping and cheering loudly, Deb sat down to listen.

Brad played with new vigor. Bradley and Deb were as different as night and day, but they always supported each other.

It was not until 9:00 p.m. that car lights flashed from the driveway.

Seeing the lights, Brad said, "I've had enough. That was great, thanks."

"My pleasure. I'll get an autograph now if you don't mind, kind sir," Deb teased.

"Why sure, here you go," Brad said as he tried to write on Deb's forehead.

With the guitar all packed up and hid away, Brad and Deb awaited some parent to walk through the door. But it was only a car using their driveway to turn around in the street.

* * *

"That was a good game we played, Rosa," Sarah said as they climbed in the car to drive home.

"What are these pills on the floor here?" Sarah asked as she reached to the floor of the car.

"Oh, they're mine," Rosa said.

"How long you have been on these? They're antidepressants, aren't they?" Sarah put the packet on the dashboard.

"Yes, about three years off and on, but they're not working too well," Rosa said.

"Oh, that reminds me. Do you remember Sally Ryan?"

Rosa nodded. "Sally Ryan. Yes, poor thing. Her life must be hell."

"Well, not any more. I saw her today and she was positively glowing."

"You don't say. What happened to her?"

"Well she said apparently she got help from this guy and she has just turned it all around."

"Really?"

"Yeah, my Lyn is going to see him next Thursday to see if

he can help her with her confidence in singing. You know she gets real bad stage fright."

"No, I didn't know that."

"Yeah, well, Sally was helped so we'll see what he can do for Lyn."

"That's interesting, let me know how it goes. Who is this guy?"

"I can give you his number if you want. I'll give it to Lyn to give to Deb."

"No, don't bother; it's not that important. Just let me know how it goes first. It sounds too good to be true."

As Rosa dropped Sarah off, she noticed that her car's windscreen had been smashed. "What happened to your car?"

"Some vandals must have smashed it last night," Sarah said.

"I hope they don't come around to our place."

"Yes, me too. Bye, Rosa."

"Bye, Sarah."

Upon arriving home, Rosa found fast food sitting in the fridge for her to eat. Fred was watching television and the kids were in their rooms.

"How did your game go? Play well?" Fred asked, his eyes still glued to the television, a beer in his hand, and a few cans on the table next to him.

Rosa just grunted at him.

"Listen, I'd like to apologize for the way I spoke to you last night, I was out of line when I—"

"Good night," Rosa said as she cut him off. She'd heard it all before.

Fine, Fred thought to himself. *See if I bother apologizing again. I can't seem to please her no matter what I do. I think I'll see what Pam's doing tonight.*

Fred grabbed his car keys and headed out the door. As he backed out of the garage, he briefly thought he shouldn't be driving after having so much to drink. He put the thought out of his head and headed for Pam's place. As he drove, he started to weave and then crossed the center line.

Fred swerved back into his lane and managed to drive mostly straight the rest of the way. When he arrived at Pam's place, he knocked on the door and let himself in.

"Hey, beautiful," he slurred, walking over to where she sat on the couch. "I sure could use some lovin' tonight."

She looked at him with a mixture of pity and resignation. No matter how many times she tried to cut off their relationship, she always gave in.

"Hi, Fred. What's wrong?"

"Nothing's wrong, I just missed you."

"You've been drinking again. Do you think you should've driven all the way over here like that?"

"What, are you going to start nagging me, too? What's the matter with you, women? Why can't you just leave me alone and accept me for who I am?"

He sat down on the couch next to her. "I'm an important person. I'm your boss. You should respect me."

"Honey, it's okay, I didn't mean anything by it. I just didn't want to see you get hurt."

Already forgetting what she was talking about, he slid next to her and tried kissing her. She responded hesitantly, and then gave in and kissed him back.

Fred left Pam's place a couple hours later and slowly started driving home. He'd had a few more beers with Pam and was feeling drunk and tired. He struggled to keep his eyes open, but it became increasingly difficult. Crossing an intersection, he realized that the light had turned red and he should have stopped. The last thing he remembered was hearing the screeching of brakes and bright lights coming straight for him.

* * *

Rosa heard the phone ringing, but thanks to her sleeping

medication, she could barely move. Eventually she was able to grab the phone and groggily said, "Hello."

"Mrs. Murray?"

"Yes. Who is this?"

"This is the police. Your husband has been in an accident and—"

"What?" Rosa was fully awake now. "What happened? Is he okay? Where is he?"

"Calm down, Mrs. Murray. Your husband is going to be okay. He's at the emergency room and should be released in about an hour. He was drinking, however, so we'll need to take him to jail. He'll see a judge in the morning and will probably be released after that, and then you can bring him home. Also, his car was wrecked; we'll need you to sign a release form."

After hanging up, Rosa couldn't sleep and went to the kitchen to make something to eat. The noise woke up her children and soon Deb and Brad were up, also.

"Hey, Mom, what's up? What are you doing up so late?" Brad asked.

"It's your father. He was in an accident and—"

"Is he okay?" Deb said, a bit of panic in her voice.

"Yes, he's fine, but he was drinking and they're taking him to jail."

"Nice," Brad said. "What a great role model. What was he doing out so late, anyway?"

Rosa looked away and said, "I don't know."

Deb and Brad looked at each other. Like their mother, they suspected what their dad was up to, but didn't want to say it aloud.

***

The next morning, Rosa slept in and both Deb and Brad took the bus to school. As they got on the bus, the same man that Deb nearly sat on the previous day got on after and sat in the seat in front of them. Deb nudged Brad and whispered,

"That's the guy I was telling you about. I don't know what it is, but there's something about him. I haven't talked to him; I don't even know his name."

Brad leaned forward and tapped the man on the shoulder, while Deb hissed, "Don't!"

"Excuse me, sir," Brad said. "My name is Brad and this is my sister, Deb. What's your name?"

"Well, hi there," the man said. "My name is Frank. It's very nice to meet you. Are you two skipping school today?"

"No, we're not skipping school," said Brad. "We're on our way there right now. Our dad was thrown in jail last night and our mom slept in—again—and we're kind of on our own these days."

"Brad!" Deb hissed again. "Shut up!"

"That's too bad," Frank said. "It can be hard to keep it together when your family's falling apart. I'm proud of you for keeping at school."

"Oh, we're not falling apart," Deb said. "Dad has a good job and Mom rarely sleeps in. Don't pay attention to Brad."

"Oh really," Brad said. "Is that why Mom is on anti-depressants and sleeping meds and cries all the time and fights with Dad because he drinks too much every night?"

"Brad, stop it, that's not anybody else's business."

"Well," Frank said, "I'll let you two get back to your conversation."

"What's that book you're reading?" Brad said.

"It's called *Destiny's Highway—In My Heart, I Shine, I Am My Strength* and it's by a guy by the name of Michael Quirk. He's a local author, actually. He has an office just a few blocks from here. He changed my life."

"Really? How'd he do that?" Brad asked.

"That's a long story," Frank said, "and my bus stop is coming up. Have a great day at school."

* * *

Rosa woke up late and called out for the kids, but when

there was no answer, she looked at her phone and saw it was almost 11:00 a.m. She called in sick to work and drove downtown to pick up Fred. When she found out he still hadn't seen the judge, she walked a couple of blocks to get something to eat. Walking into the restaurant, she saw Pam sitting alone at a table and walked over.

"Hi, Pam," Rosa said. "On lunch break?"

"Hi, Rosa. The boss isn't in today, so I took an early lunch. Don't tell him," she said and winked.

"You didn't hear?" Rosa said. "Fred was in an accident last night."

"What?" Pam said, and then hesitated. "What happened?"

"He was out somewhere drinking and got hit crossing an intersection. He's fine, but the police kept him in jail overnight because he was drunk. He had to see the judge this morning, but should be done soon. I came down to pick him up, but he wasn't ready yet."

Pam looked away and then turned back to Rosa. "How are you doing?" she said.

"I'm tired," Rosa said. "Tired of his drinking, tired of his yelling, tired of everything."

Pam stood up quickly. "I need to get back to work. I hope everything turns out okay. Tell Mr. Murray that I'll be at work the rest of the day, so if he needs anything..."

Rosa stared at her as she walked away and wondered if her suspicions were right. No longer hungry, she left to see if her husband was finally out of jail.

**

Fred was waiting as she drove up, and she quickly picked him up and started driving.

"Where do you want to go?" she said.

"Work, of course. Do you think that place will run itself without me?"

Neither one talked the rest of the way there and when

she dropped him off, she said, "I'll be back to pick you up at five."

"Can you make it seven? I have a lot to catch up on."

"No, I have a basketball game tonight. I'll see you at six and if you're not ready, maybe Pam can give you a ride home."

He quickly got out of the car and said, "See you at six."

Rosa drove home and wondered if her life could get any worse.

* * *

Fred walked into work as if nothing had happened. He asked Pam to come into his office and update him about what had happened so far that morning. She gave him an odd look and then walked into his office behind him.

Fred sat at his desk and Pam sat in the chair opposite and they looked at each other for a few minutes before Fred said, "Well, what's happened that I need to know about?"

"Fred, are you okay?" Pam said.

"Of course I'm okay; I just want to know if I have any calls to return or fires to put out."

"But what about last night?"

"Last night has nothing to do with the work I need to get done," Fred said. "If you don't have any updates, then I need to get to work." He turned his computer on and started going through papers while Pam hesitated and then walked out of his office.

"What the hell," she muttered under her breath.

* * *

When Rosa got back home, she collapsed on her bed and started to cry. She knew Fred was cheating on her with his secretary and she ached with the pain of it. She took several sleeping pills and then fell into an oblivion where she felt no pain.

Destiny's Highway

* * *

Pam refused to talk to Fred for the rest of the day. She left at the end of the day without saying a word and slammed the door on her way out. Six came and went and Rosa didn't come to pick him up.

"Damn women," Fred muttered. He walked to the bus stop and got on the next bus that went past his house. The bus was full, but there was one seat left next to a man reading a book titled *Destiny's Highway*. He sat down and tried to not think about the day or the night before. When he got home, he poured himself a drink and then sat down to watch sports on the television.

Chapter 6

Sarah picked Lyn up from school on Thursday afternoon so they would arrive on time for their appointment. They were the only two in the waiting room.

"Mom, I'm really nervous," Lyn whispered to her mom. "Can we go home?"

"No, darling, you'll be all right."

They didn't have to wait long before Michael opened the door.

"Hello folks, it's Lyn and Sarah—yes?"

"Yes, that's right."

"Come on in."

"Hello, I'm Michael," he said, holding out his hand to Sarah.

Sarah shook hands, and Lyn followed suit.

They walked into his office; there was a small desk, a few desk chairs, office stuff, and a big reclining chair.

"Do you want me to stay or go, dear?" Sarah asked.

"Can you stay?" pleaded Lyn.

"Is that all right?" asked Sarah as she looked at Michael.

"Whatever she likes, sure."

"How about you sit here at the desk, Lyn, and your mom can sit beside you."

Michael sat on the other side of the small desk.

"It is lovely and quiet here. You can hear the bellbirds," Sarah commented.

"You can, the bush is right here," replied Michael. "Where do you live, Lyn?"

"14 Federation Drive, Turret Ville," she told him and he started filling out a record card.

"What's it like living there?"

"Fine."

"Do you have any brothers or sisters?"

"No."

"Where do you go to school?"

"At St. Cecilia's at Bradbeach."

"That's a fair way to travel, how do you get there from your place?"

"I've got a friend, Deb, who lives nearby and we catch the bus to Fairview, then we catch another bus to school."

"What's that like?"

"Fine."

"So what brings you along today? Why are you here?"

Lyn began to struggle and Michael could see she was guarding her speech. "Well, because I can't sing as well as I want to and—my teacher—wants me to go—in singing competitions and I can't do it," replied Lyn.

"And..." prompted her mother.

"What!" Lyn exclaimed.

"You get sick a lot," Sarah added.

"Oh yeah, I get sick a lot and we were wondering if you could help that because you helped Mrs. Ryan."

"Okay. What do you mean by sick a lot?"

"Well, the last time I was sick, last week, that's when Mom called you. Before that..." she trailed off and looked at her mother.

Sarah chimed in. "Lyn would be sick at least once a month. Sometimes she goes to school and other times she doesn't. The other thing is her singing teacher has wanted her to go in concerts for the last two years and each time she gets sick. She'll throw up and get a headache."

"Yeah, that's about it," said Lyn.

"How are you feeling right now, Lyn?"

"I'm fine."

"What does fine mean?"

"Just the usual, I suppose." She looked quizzically at Michael.

"How's your stomach and your head?"

Lyn paused for a while and said, "My head is a bit tight and my stomach is a bit sick."

"Do you know what you're feeling, what your emotions are right now? Like, are you frightened, nervous or sad?"

"Not really."

"But you know when you're feeling good and feeling bad?"

"Yes."

"That's good! So let's talk about the different parts of you. There's a part that wants to sing in a concert? Yes?"

"Yes," Lyn nodded

"And there's a different part that doesn't?"

"Yes." Lyn nodded again

"There's a part that does want to go to school? And there's a part that doesn't?"

"Yes."

"Let's look at the part that doesn't. Let's call that the feeling part. And let's put 'innocent Lyn' in there, because that's where she lives. If I say 'innocent Lyn' to you, what comes to you? Does any part of your life come to you, at any age?"

Lyn looked away and stared across the room and said, "Yes."

"Where is she?"

"Going to pre-school."

"Can you see her?"

"Yes."

"What is she doing?"

Tears came to her eyes.

"It's okay, Lyn," he said as he offered her a tissue, "just let her be with you and feel her," Michael reassured.

"She's playing; she's make-believe singing with a stick as a microphone in the playground at pre-school. And everyone's laughing at her."

"How is she feeling?"

"Sad." Tears began to run down her face.

"Now Lyn, if that innocent girl came through that door," Michael pointed to the door into the room, "right now, what would you do?"

"I'd give her a hug," she said.

"Yes, you would. But she is here, now, right with you, because you can feel her. She is here. And your 15-year-old Lyn can hold her right now. And you will because you can feel how sad she is. It's the sadness that makes you want to hold her, so it's the sadness that makes you love her. Go ahead and hold her right now and let's see what happens."

After a minute or two, Lyn had tears rolling down her cheeks, but she was smiling as well. She had a smile on her face as she was crying.

"Weird, isn't it. How weird is that?" Michael said. "How can you be so sad and yet feel so good?"

Lyn looked at her mother who was starting to cry as well.

"So Mom's innocent girl—innocent Sarah—has come to join us. Well, right now you both have a point of power, at a point of change. Are you going to tell yourself to pull yourself together and don't be a sook or whatever you say to yourself to hold it in?"

Lyn joined in. "Don't be an idiot, get a grip! That's what I say to myself."

"Yeah that's it, all that stuff," replied Michael. "Or are you going to let empathetic Lyn and empathetic Sarah start to run the show?"

"Can you feel the difference between being harsh and judgmental versus gentle empathy? We need to begin with the gentleness, the empathy. That's what Love wants us to do to ourselves. Never in a million years does the coping logic know that sadness is warmth. Sadness is the part of you that tells you that 'this is not good enough.' Sadness is love talking to you.

"Just now Lyn, you've just done the opposite of what the coping tells you to do—block it off and make out that it's not there. It tells you that it's a terrible place to go because it feels so bad. But when you go there with empathy, it turns the black coal into white electricity. That's how you laugh and cry at the same time. That particular part of you is now no longer disconnected from you. You start to connect with yourself.

"That's the process that you've begun today, and if you want, it will continue and it goes where it goes. Empathy works like putting a drop of dye in a bucket of water; all you have to do is begin and eventually it will spread throughout.

"We go to the age of innocence because it's easy to empathize with an innocent child. All that harsh, judgmental stuff doesn't apply. It can't 'belt up' an innocent child because she is just that—innocent. If you feel how sad she is, you cannot judge her, so it's easy to be empathetic. With most people we need the innocence to begin the empathy, because when you're older your judgment will come in and say such things as 'you're old enough to know better, pull yourself together!' What you did just then, turned the sadness to warmth with empathy is the beginning of what we're on about.

"At this stage, that's what we're doing in a nutshell. So what I would like you to do is stay with her as much as you can. If I see you in a week or so, I would like you to take that girl by the hand with you wherever you go. In the meantime, treat yourself as if you were her, an innocent child. Any time you lose or forget her, she'll make you feel sad again, so you'll get her back again. Do you understand?"

"Yes, I think so," said Lyn and Sarah in unison.

"Now, if I said to you, 'it's as simple as that,' you wouldn't believe me. But it is. On the one hand, on the feeling level, it's simple. But on the thinking level, and you don't get it, it's complex. You can go into a complicated maze of thinking and analysis, have a brain snap, and come out with no answers and no relief. That coping side will never be able to give you that feeling that you just generated by yourself for yourself. How good is that? I reckon that's magic, there's no feeling like it. What do you think? We've just shown your logic something that it didn't know—how to generate love for yourself."

"I feel great. Like clearer, fresh even, but mellow at the same time, sort of sad but not bad sad," Lyn reported

"That's it. Have you still got that innocent girl with you?"

"Yes," she said, "she is sitting on my lap."

"Great. Now instead of trying to push her away, she's come to you to show you something. She wants you to rescue her from that place and in doing so she has come to rescue you. Let go and be with her in her world and feel things with her."

Another wave of sadness welled up inside of Lyn. "She's having fun, but they're laughing at her."

"Who's laughing at her?"

"The other kids. One boy calls me stupid, he's saying 'look at her' and laughing. She throws her stick away and runs and cries in the bathroom." As Lyn relived the events of the past, she reported in the first person and in the third person, fluctuating between the two.

"But I hit my head on the door as she went inside, still crying. My head is hurting but she's too scared to cry out." Another wave of sadness. "So she has to hold it in because she doesn't want to be found. Nobody knows, I don't want anyone to find me."

Feeling with her daughter and in tears, Sarah said to Lyn, "But you never told me, I never knew," as she looked across at Michael.

"It was meant to be like that. I'll explain in a while, I want to just stay with Lyn." Michael continued.

"Here is this little innocent girl. She feels frightened, hurt, alone, and sad. With no one to help her except you right here, right now. You're empathetic Lyn, fifteen, in this chair with your arms around her right here today. You can help her because you're the only one that knows how she is really feeling. You can feel right now how she felt then because the feelings are the same. They haven't gone away, no matter how much time has gone. That's twelve years ago and the feelings are as fresh as the day it happened. Am I right, Lyn?"

"Yes, they are."

"That's amazing," said Sarah. "How are you doing?" she asked Lyn.

"Good, good," replied Lyn.

"So we can say then that in the innocent little girl's eye, 'the world is a scary place.' People only hurt you. She feels sad, alone—unworthy, if you like. And her head hurts."

"Yes."

"Are these feelings familiar to you, Lyn? How many times have you felt like that?"

"Lots of times."

"Especially when you are supposed to perform in some way," Michael added.

"Yes."

"This is what we think happens. We think that these outside events are making us feel this way. Initially, in our innocence, we lock in a perspective. It doesn't have to be real; it could be just the way the innocence felt it to be. From then on, it'll create situations to make you feel the same way again and again. You see, the innocence is so powerless and yet so powerful. As adults, we think that something happens that has caused us to feel the way we feel. Not so. At this stage, let's say a part of you has had a hand in determining the events that you have walked into today and every day, to show you how you're really feeling. So you can then empathize with them and turn them to warmth. That's what love wants you to do. Magic happens every day. Unworthiness creates unworthiness everywhere with everyone, despite all the best coping techniques there are."

Another wave of sadness came over Lyn.

"Put your arms around her, reassure her, talk to her. Remember, you're the only person that knows how she's feeling. Empathetic Lyn, you are the only one that can help her."

"I'm not there now, I've gone to when I'm older," reported Lyn.

"Oh, welcome, older Lyn. What would you like to show big Lyn?" Michael asked.

"This time I'm at primary school and I'm being teased by these boys. One of the boys, it's the same kid at pre-school. Yeah, Billy was his name. He never let up on me. Just about every day he would have a go at me. I always stayed on the other side of the playground so he wouldn't come near me.

"Here's another one. This was only three years ago. I was supposed to read in front of class, so I played up, and I'd been sent outside so I wouldn't have to read." Lyn was experiencing the memories unravelling inside of her.

"Do you see some of the coping things you do to try and stop feeling bad, exactly the same as the little girl in pre-school?" asked Michael

"Yes."

"Do you see that all the coping things that you've done have never taken this feeling away? They haven't worked and they won't ever work, because the innocence and love is too strong."

"Yes, yes."

"But now you have a group of Lyns with empathetic Lyn's arms around all of them. How does that feel?"

"Really good."

"Excellent work, Lyn. And each one of those times the girl has been trying to reach you, and each time you've probably called yourself an idiot. No wonder the girl is lonely. But what happens when you listen to her feelings, you're listening to her voice. Your feelings are her voice; they're the language of the innocence. If you don't listen to her, she has no one.

The more you block her off, the more she has to do things to get your attention. The more things she has to manifest in reality to get you to feel today the way she feels. If you feel today what she's feeling, sadness and unworthiness, then you'll be able to empathize and hence love her. But the more we cope, the more we move away from her. She'll bring you back to her. The situations she creates will be more and more severe. You'll get to the point where you won't be able to cope anymore or you can't cope anymore.

"If that's what it takes for you to feel her, then so be it. You'll learn to love yourself. That's her gift to you. Embrace the feelings that you bottle up. It's up to you. That's the way love works, you can't beat it, it's the gravity of the feeling world. It has a reason for everything—for you to feel what love is. And within the universal limits you'll see that part of you is like a director in your reality. We'll go over this as many times as you wish as you go along. Don't worry about taking it all in, now. You have felt the warmth, that's the main thing. You've begun."

"Yeah."

"So calling yourself an idiot helps?"

Lyn laughed and said, "No!"

"But you've done it so many times."

"Yes, I know."

"Maybe you haven't done it long enough. Maybe it hasn't got through to you yet. Maybe if you give yourself another three weeks to call yourself an idiot, maybe that will help. No, let's be fair. Let's give it another ten years—that should work. Do you get the picture, Lyn? Coping, judgment, and righteousness don't know how feelings work. Love is way ahead of them.

"Now let me tell you of the power you have. You know love has an agenda. Firstly, it wants us to understand what love is. It's a feeling. If you're not feeling and trying to stop yourself from feeling, then that's like trying to stop gravity. You have no chance. Things will become diseased. Love is urging you to feel as quickly as possible so you will feel good as quickly as possible.

"Your life force is like a stream coming down a mountainside. When it comes to a waterfall, the water is supposed to go over the cliff and keep going, but the coping part of you blocks it off and stops it from going over. It builds the water up. If you like, the coping part builds a gate like a dam to stop the feelings flowing through you. The coping part then redirects the water back into the hillside into a series of stagnant ponds, which are the things you do to try and cope.

"Now today we brought in empathetic Lyn. She says, 'Look, I already know you're coping and you're struggling. I know you don't know who you are and what you're doing. That's all right. So why don't I crack the gate open and you can feel what you're feeling and then you'll find out who you are, what love is, and what you can do with it for the rest of your life? It takes a lot of energy to hold the water back, that's why depressed people are like the walking dead. But it takes no energy to let it go.

"Love has set it up so that everything in your life is on a video recording; you have a whole reservoir of experiences that you've felt to know what love is not. However, when you empathize with those feelings, they change to what love is and that's how you love yourself and that's the whole point of it all. Do you sort of get it?

"I think so."

"Let me tell you about the power of your feelings. It is sort of like this. They work like a slide projector. Whatever slide you put into the projector, that's the picture you get on the screen. What you feel in your innocence is the slide. What these feelings create is the picture; your reality is on the screen. If you want to change reality, you need to change the slide. This means if you try to change the way you feel by changing reality, you will end up in futility.

"It's like trying to paint a different picture on the projecting screen with a paintbrush. The light from the projector will go over the paint and show the picture that's on the slide. Maybe you can already see in your life that unworthiness has put you in or has determined that you will and have been in unworthy situations. As you work with the process and when the empathy has strengthened, the sadness changes to warmth. The unworthiness changes to worthiness and you'll see later on how that then determines your new worthy reality. Love shows you that within limits, what you feel determines what you create.

"Do you see that innocent little girl has been trapped in that place since you left her there and you've been trying to cope ever since? But the power of your feelings, the girl and love want you to learn what love is. By empathizing with the girl today, you've begun. Have you still got the group of Lyns with you?"

"Yes. There is something else, though."

"What's that?"

"I'm due to do a math test tomorrow. I usually get flustered and blow it on silly mistakes. I know the work but come exam time, I can't do it as well."

"So let's bring in the girl right here now who's going to do a math exam. How does she feel?"

"The same as the others, nervous."

"Let's bring her in the group with the others and embrace her, too."

"How is she?" he asked.

"Still a bit frightened."

"Stay with her from now on and you'll feel the difference. Other Lyn's will continue to come now. Your empathetic self will give them the time until they feel safe and warm with you. The more empathy there is, the stronger you'll feel. Don't underestimate 'the judger,' it will not go away until you're strong enough".

"Today we've seen that you have three parts.

"The Feeling part, where you met 'innocent Lyn' and the other Lyns. You learned that feelings don't know time.

The feelings are there as if it was today. When the logic says the past is the past and get over it, it doesn't know what it's talking about as far as the feelings are concerned. The innocent girl is still down the hole, sad and alone. The only way to rescue her is with—

"The Empathetic part. She's in opposition to the judgmental—

"Righteous part that calls her an idiot and blocks her off.

"We've learned when we're empathetic to ourselves Sadness is Warmth.

"That's about if for today. Do you have any questions?" Michael said, looking at both Lyn and Sarah.

"No, but I want to make an appointment. And I'll try and bring my husband along as well. We've been having a few problems. Do you deal with couples?" Sarah asked "Do you want to come again, Lyn?"

"Yes, I do," said Lyn.

"Yes, I deal with couples," replied Michael.

"Good, I'll make an appointment."

If Lyn had come to see me years before I would have helped her in the following manner:

I would have explained to her that we wanted to teach her a relaxation response to being on stage and when doing exams, because we have two specific situations to which she is frightened.

I'd teach her relaxation and she'd practice at home so she could feel what that was like. In this state of relaxation, we'd go through a hierarchy of situations that Lyn was frightened of. For example, with her exams, we'd start out with Lyn being in a peaceful place so she could feel relaxed. Then she'd imagine going to a place where she first hears that she'll be having an exam and she'd feel that fear from that scene. We'd release the fear by breathing until she felt relaxed again about the exam. This might have to be done many times until she felt relaxed. Then we'd proceed through to a next scene like the morning of the exam. We'd work through a series of events leading up to the exam itself until she'd be in the exam focused and relaxed and working at her optimum efficiently.

The same process would be applied to her stage fright.

In dealing with Lyn's fear in this way, fear is looked upon as some unneeded response, some ancient evolution emotion that's gotten in the way and prevents her from leading a fulfilling life. We need to eradicate it and get it out of the way or we need to overcome it. It's treated as if it's a mistake, a part of Lyn that is a cancer and needs to be cut out.

This process will help her cope with her problems, but the fear will probably resurface in the same way or some other way. Like a water tank that springs a leak is patched, it'll only spring a leak somewhere else. Love looks at what the leaks are saying, rather than just fixing them. From love's perspective, fear has a purpose. In nature, nothing is for nothing.

For us to find love, we need to have the capacity to feel emotions. We can feel fear easily because our evolution has been built on it. It's been around a long time. It can scare us off, we can begin to feel using fear. If we block it off and deem it unnecessary, then we block off our ability to feel other feelings as well as love. Love shows us first what love is not. Feel what it's not, then empathize with it and you'll then feel what love is.

Lyn has not found the love within herself and that's what the Love agenda wants. Her fear is trying to show her that and the subsequent reality that the fear is creating in her face is trying to show her that as well. All roads lead to Rome. Eventually, Lyn will have to come back to herself, feel her fear as a pathway to feeling her sadness and then empathize with herself to feel the warmth. Then her fear won't have to show itself in exams or on stage or in any other way.

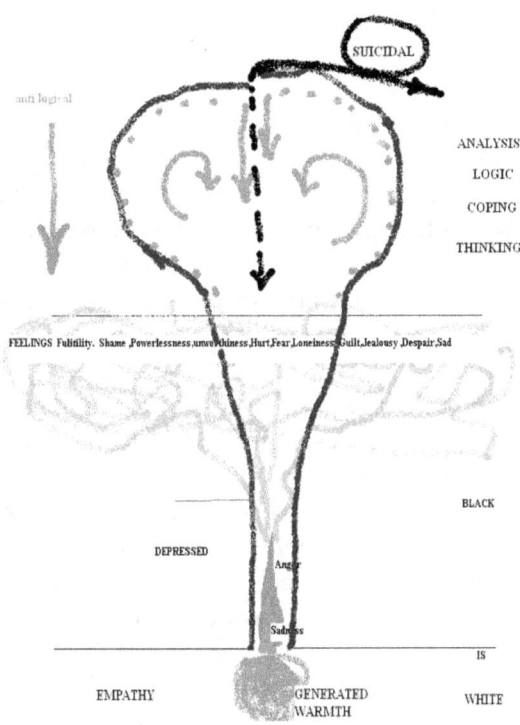

The hottest part of a fire is the blue flame.
This is where the sadness is.
This is where we can convert the sadness to warmth.
This is where the innocent child lives.
Around that is the red flame.
This is anger.

Heat and smoke come from the flame, which has all the other feelings in the feeling world. Fear, pain, sadness, despair, futility, jealousy, powerlessness, guilt, shame, and frustration.

We don't want to live in this world because we're taught feelings are weak, ugly, and unreliable. We're not encouraged to live with them, so we block them off and we go out into Coping Land, where we use thinking, analyzing, and logic. We judge in a big way. Righteousness is very strong.

Now love and the universal agenda have decided that our purpose here is to learn what love is by learning to love ourselves. Then to see that we are creators because we've already created our world on unworthiness. If we change the sadness to warmth, we can manifest that warmth and fulfill our destiny. So the first part in that scenario is to feel. Everyone can feel fear, sadness, loneliness, and unworthiness. Open the door to the feeling world and you open the door to love because black is white.

But the coping part has a man-made agenda and part of the man-made agenda is that feelings don't matter, so the more you move away from your feelings and go out into virtual reality, the more you'll struggle because the unworthiness is undermining your struggle to gain happiness outside of yourself. The more you move away from your feelings of sadness, the more you will feel sad. This can be called depression. You pick yourself up and continue to cope again only to be brought back to the sadness again. We have coping patterns and all them end in futility. It's logical to think we have to cope, but in order to solve our problems we have to do an illogical thing by embracing the feelings with empathy. If we do, we can change the reality we manifest on the screen, instead of trying to cover it. That's the power of empathy. That's the power of us.

How do you know that you're doing it right?

If you're feeling sad, warm and mellow. If you're crying with a smile on your face. If you're doing that then you're embracing yourself with empathy. You can feel the warmth. It's automatic.

If you're sad and crying, but as a result feel worse, then you'll be judging yourself in some way. In that case, always bring in your innocence—you can't judge an innocent child.

Sarah and Lyn were enjoying their time together after

leaving Michael's. They both helped each other by saying things like, "And how is innocent Sarah doing?"

"She's with me, and how is innocent Lyn going?"

"She's with me, singing again, and she's enjoying it," Lyn would answer.

When James came home that night, both Lyn and Sarah were in such a happy mood he wanted to know the story.

"What's with you two?" James asked.

"Dad, you know I was going to see someone about me getting sick?" chirped Lyn.

"Yes, sort of," James replied.

"Well, it was great! It wasn't like I thought it'd be. We did stuff, and it felt really good."

Sarah joined in. "That's right, love. This is different from what we got at counseling when we went before."

"That wasn't much help, they only told us what we already knew and she made out like it was my entire fault anyway. I'm not going back again," James stated clearly.

"I'm going to see this Michael for me," Sarah said, "and it would be great if you were to as well. After all, don't you think the guy who smashed my car windscreen last week needs some help?" Sarah looked at James.

"That was bad. Bloody hopeless, I certainly lost it," James said, putting his head down.

"Dad, you freaked me out, please get some help. You'll like this guy, he doesn't judge you, he doesn't analyze you, he just shows you stuff. It's really cool," Lyn urged.

"Listen, I want to work this out. I don't like getting angry all the time."

"You'll only end up wrecking more things, including yourself, if you don't solve this thing!" Sarah pleaded. "I made a time late in the day hoping you'd come. Why don't you come with me?"

"Okay. Why not?" James agreed.

"Yes!" Sarah and Lyn said in unison.

"What's it about?" James asked

Both Lyn and Sarah told James it was about looking after yourself as if you were innocent to begin with. You cry, but you smile at the same time.

"I find that hard to believe."

"You'll see. We'll leave it to you to talk to Michael yourself. He'll explain it to you, and you can ask questions."

"Fair enough. If it's that good I'm looking forward to it." James changed the subject, "What's for dinner?"

Lyn knew her work for the math exam that she was having the next day, but she always messed the exam up—she sabotaged herself. Then, when she received her marked exam paper back with the usual low mark, she'd review her exam. This involved criticizing herself for being an idiot over and over again, for making the silly mistakes that she did. Usually when she went to bed she would hear a voice in her head telling her how stupid she was, then she'd have trouble going to sleep and have a restless night. She'd wake up tired, then would hassle herself for not getting a good night's sleep, thus putting more pressure on herself for the next day.

That night Lyn went to sleep with innocent Lyn and the other Lyns snuggled up beside her. She had a restful night's sleep and woke up refreshed. She felt a little anxious, but not that bad.

The next day Deb arrived at Lyn's place for school. Lyn was up and about ready for school. "Are you ready for the math exam today, Lyn?" Deb called out. This was really a question with a hidden agenda. Deb knew that Lyn always did poorly on the exam, so she thought she would twist the knife a little. Getting better exam results compared to Lyn always went well for Deb's ego.

"Sure. I'm fine. Part of me is actually looking forward to it," Lyn said.

"Really? That's good; let's go," said Deb, but thought to herself, *That's weird. She should be nervous as hell.*

Chapter 7

A few days later, Fred had just settled into his office when Pam called out, "Mr. Murray, Schofields is on the line."

Fred took the call in his office. "How are you, Schofields? How are things?"

"Not good, Mr. Murray. Listen I'm going to give you my notice. I've decided to stay up here and look after my mom. I'll only be back to pick up my things next week and then I'll be staying here." Schofields told the story very convincingly.

"I'm sorry to hear that, Schofields. You're a good man to work with, but your family must come first. Of course, it's the right thing to do; I'll see you when you come down and collect your things. Bye for now."

"Okay, Mr. Murray. Bye for now."

No sooner did he hang up the phone before he heard Pam's voice again. "Mr. Murray, Barry Heaton is waiting on line one."

"Hello, Barry, how's the drama going at home?" asked Fred.

"Don't want to talk about it. I'm taking the bitch to court, and she's taking me to court; the solicitors are trying to work something out. So how are things in the business, Fred?" inquired Barry, knowing Schofields had left.

"Schofields just left and is moving interstate to look after his sick mother, so now I have to find someone to replace him."

"Is that right? Listen Fred, I've decided to take a step back a bit. I'm at the point where I don't know why I'm doing what I'm doing. Things don't seem right anymore, hard to explain, maybe a mid-life crisis? I'm making money. My businesses are going fine. I'm a consultant to the financial departments in two other states. I'm on the board of three companies and right now I think I've got enough on my plate with these personal hassles as well. I'm going to take a break. I might go away somewhere and chill out for a while. So what I'm saying is you won't be able to contact me until I contact you," explained Barry.

"Are you sure, Barry? I could really use your advice about—"

"Okay, then, I'll see you when I see you." Barry ended the conversation.

By the time Fred had got off the phone it was after 5:00 p.m. and everyone had already gone home, even Pam. To Fred, the sign on the wall that said, "When the going gets tough, the tough get going," seemed a bit meaningless. He'd have to muster all his strength to overcome all his problems: no manager, sales dropping, no partner available, and no money to pull the business out of trouble.

Feeling totally dejected, even his best motivational material was struggling and was even useless against the feelings Fred had now. He wanted to seek comfort in a place that was convenient to him—in the arms of Pam—but she was barely talking to him. Also, he had no car and had to take the bus home. He kept a bottle of vodka in the back of his bottom drawer in the filing cabinet and decided to spend some time with the only friend that never let him down.

* * *

It was the time of Barry Heaton's first appointment to see Michael.

"Come on in, Barry. My name is Michael. What can I help you with?"

"Well, I went to my doctor with some problems and he advised me to come and have a talk with you."

"Sure." After taking down some particulars, Michael asked whether Barry was married.

"No such luck. Let's just say I've had a bit of trouble with women through my life. That's what's brought me here.'

"Really, what sort of trouble?"

"Well, the last one charged me with assault after I had to pin her down so she wouldn't wreck the rest of my house and belongings. She called the police and told them some bull story, even after I treated her so well. I'd taken her in, she had nothing, bought her a car, paid for her mother's unit and got her useless brother a job at one of my businesses, even though he's hopeless. Oh, it goes on and on.

"The one before that used to drink too much and accused me of sleeping around. She was bad news. I've lost count of how many. I've had enough, I can't sleep, can't function at work.

"You know, I'm pretty successful, but I'm at the point where I don't know why I'm doing what I'm doing. My businesses are making plenty of money. I'm well respected on the corporate level. Businesses and governments use me as a consultant. I'm on the board of three companies, and right now I feel overwhelmed. Now with this hassle as well, it's too much. I think I need to take a break. I was thinking about going away somewhere and taking a rest for a while.

"I'm 51 years old. Never been married, no kids. Free to do what I want when I want. I've done everything I'm supposed to do, but I'm not happy. Excuse the French, but I feel like shit. To tell you the truth, this latest affair has rocked me. I mean, I'm a high flying businessman. I don't get shook up by anything. Well, I'm not supposed to, but this woman has knocked me off my perch. If I weren't a coward, I'd end it all. There are times when, honestly, that's how I really feel."

"Barry, you're to be congratulated on all your financial success. It sounds like you've done very well for yourself on one level, but not on another. Just like most people. There are always things to learn. What I can help you with is work on another level—the feeling level. That's what I can help you with, if you want. Would you like that?"

"Well, yes, I'm willing to learn," replied Barry.

"Great! Let's begin. Where do you come from originally?" asked Michael

"I was brought up in a little village in Scotland. You could say I was the little bastard of the village. I didn't know who my father was. We were dirt poor. My grandmother, Nan, brought me up mainly, because my mother used to work all the time."

"What was your grandmother like?"

"You know, things were pretty hard in those times. She had to look after my two cousins and me because they had lost their parents. She was a pretty hard woman, but she did the best she could."

"So did you get any nurturing at all? Who gave you cuddles and warmth and such?" Michael asked.

"Nobody. Never got that. All I got was a clip behind the ear, mostly every day. I had to spend some time in an orphanage for about three months at a time. Yeah, used to be put into that place whenever Nan wanted a rest, or because my mother was ill. That's when I first went there. I was about eight or so."

"Do you remember that?"

"I can still see the iron gates of that place."

"Can you feel what you were feeling then?"

Tears started to well up in his eyes. "Sorry, Michael."

"Don't be sorry, Barry, you have a boy here who needs your help. Can you see him?"

"I see him every time. I can't sleep and he won't go away."

"Well, let's say he wants you to help him. That's why you still see him."

"But how can I do that? The past is the past, I've gotten on with it. I couldn't go moping around and cry about it. I wasn't allowed to anyway, Nan would have seen to that. I had to get on with my life."

"And you have, but where does that leave the boy? In the same place as you left him. You've heard the expression about bottling your feelings up?"

"Yes, of course."

"If you put something in a bottle a long time ago and haven't poured it out of the bottle then where does that leave it?"

"Still in the bottle," replied Barry. "But when I was a kid, Nan would clip me around the ear if I whined or complained or didn't eat my shit dinner."

"Barry, you didn't have a say, did you? You were absolutely powerless. You were totally innocent. True?"

"Well, yeah, just a kid."

"But that kid, he's here now. You just felt him. Those feelings are still here. So the past is still present. Time hasn't healed you. You've kept yourself busy to try and solve these feelings, but they haven't gone away. But now we can do something with them to help him and you."

"Really? How do we do that?"

"Are you prepared to spend some time with innocent Barry, now, and go down and feel what he is feeling and rescue him?"

"How do I do that?"

"Can you still see those gates of the orphanage?"

"Yes, and the eight-year-old is standing next to them."

"How's he feeling?"

"He's all torn up!"

"Can you feel him?"

"Yes, he feels like shit, but part of me is blocking it, saying don't cry, you're not a wuss! I don't want to go there; I don't want to remember. I've spent all of my life trying to get away from those times; I don't like going there."

"That's your coping part that's helped you to survive, that's helped you to achieve all the success you have, but it can't help you here. We need to bring in an empathetic Barry. You know, the one that looks after those women—kind-hearted Barry—and get him to look after innocent Barry in the same away he looks after everyone else. Is he here, too?"

"Yes."

"He's gentle, patient and understanding, the best parent to yourself that you never had. Let's bring him in and join him up with that boy standing in front of the gates. Remember, feelings are the language of the boy. The more you feel him, the closer you get to him. Give yourself a minute and go down and feel him. Let's ask the coper to watch. We can say to the coper, 'We know how to embrace these feelings. It's a new way to approach feelings, watch and observe. Thanks for helping me to survive, but you can't do this. Just watch this!'"

As Barry went into himself, he could hardly stop himself from crying. With tears in his eyes, he said, "You poor little guy! He feels so alone, so frightened, so torn to bits. Poor little man.

"I never realized that he felt so bad. It was absolutely terrible. When Mom got sick and they took me away to the orphanage, I didn't know whether I'd see her again!"

With that, Barry could not hold back the tears anymore. "Sad, worthless, useless, powerless, hopeless—all that."

"Yes, that's him all right," Michael added. "He needs empathetic Barry to go down to him and hold him."

"I can't go to him. He won't let me near him. He's turning away."

"That's understandable, if you think about it. This entire time coping adult Barry has left him behind, he doesn't trust adults, and he doesn't trust anybody. But empathetic Barry knows that. He'll just sit down near him, hold his hand out until the little guy will eventually take it, because he can see that you really care for him.

"Just stay where you are and be there for him. Whenever

he's ready, he'll see your true colors. The innocent boy is real. He knows whether you're real or not. He knows if you're honest with yourself. As we talk, let empathetic Barry be with him. You can feel him. You know what he feels. Unworthy and miserable describe how he feels?"

"That's about it. You know I got out of that village when I was sixteen. I took off on an overseas ship. I worked my way up in the merchant navy and learned about business at the same time. There was no way I was going to be poor again."

"The fear of being poor has made you who you are?"

"That's right."

"But you still feel miserable today, even though you've done all that."

"Yes."

"How's the eight-year-old doing?"

"He's walking me along the corridors of the orphanage. He's showing me something. He's showing the rats that used to run around the place, and I can see the lady that used to run the place. She was a cruel woman." Tears filled up his eyes once again. "She used to clip me across the head, too! That's so cruel. He's sitting in a corner, I'm reaching out, but he doesn't trust me."

After a few minutes, "He's looking up at me. I feel sad. It's not a nice feeling.

"The coper," said Michael. "Let's invite him in. The empathetic Barry doesn't judge the coper or the judger."

"Yes," replied Barry "He's saying not to go there, don't do it, it'll be worse, you won't feel better, get over it, you'll crack up, you won't be able to cope, pull yourself together. Boy, oh boy, it's strong."

"Yes it is because you've given it your energy to survive for the last forty years or so. As an energy itself, it'll want to survive. Imagine this analogy. It's like Barry Corporation has been run by a judgmental chairman who sits at the head of a round table and rules. He's locked a door coming into the conference room. The door is labelled 'sadness'. Outside that door are all the Barrys who are sad and want to be rescued.

"Today we begin a corporation takeover. The chairman has been asked to step aside and watch how the company can now be run with a different energy, which is empathy. So the empathetic chairman takes the chair and opens the door labelled 'sadness'.

"The first Barry behind the door has been the eight-year-old at the orphanage. He's already approached you with caution and won't come any closer until he sees that you are empathetic Barry and not judgmental Barry. Then, when he feels safe, he'll sit in your lap and you'll be connected.

"Then the others lined up outside the door that have been waiting there all this time will come, gradually, until you've got your arms around the lot and the door is wide open and empathetic Barry is running things right here today. And that'll be reflected in the reality that those feelings will manifest for you, whatever that is.

"Do we have empathetic Barry on the job?"

"Yes, he's here."

"Can he see the innocent boy?"

"Yes."

"What is the eight-year-old doing now?"

"He's reaching out to hold my hand!" Sadness overwhelmed Barry and he started to sob.

"He's holding my hand! I'm holding his hand!"

"That's great. How do you feel?"

"Better, I feel better. Nice, I feel nice. It's not that bad anymore. He's smiling at me." Again, a wave of sadness came through. "That's good," he said with tears in his eyes and a smile on his face "That's unreal—I would never have thought that would happen. Never in a million years. That's amazing."

"It's a buzz," Michael replied. "Barry, you have just learned that sadness is warmth, that black is white. You've spent a lot of energy trying to block that part of you off. The boy is and has been trying to reach you, through your dreams and memories. He's saying have a look at this, feel this, remember this,

Destiny's Highway

and help me with this. But the coping part keeps saying, 'go away.'

"Would it be fair to say that there is a core that has always been running right through your life, this core is made up of the strong feelings of fear, abandonment, loneliness, sadness, and unworthiness? This core has never changed?"

"Yes, you're right, Michael."

Michael then drew a diagram.

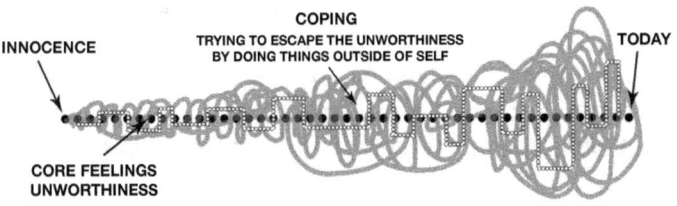

SOMETIMES YOU CAN COPE, BUT ARE ALWAYS BROUGHT BACK TO UNWORTHINESS

"The first step in empathy is that you acknowledge how you're feeling, acknowledging that you're feeling miserable. 'That's great,' says empathetic Barry, 'now you're being real. Now we can stop bullshitting ourselves and get on with loving ourselves knowing that black is really white. So knowing that you are lost is the first step in being found.

"That's the symbol Destiny's Highway," Michael said as he showed Barry the crossover symbol.

DESTINY'S

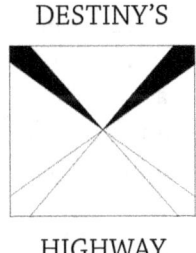

HIGHWAY

"What was strong (the thinking judger) is now weak and what was weak (the feeling empathy) is now strong. At the crossover point is where you are now. At this point there will be plenty of times when you'll be confused and uncertain about things. That's because you are going from what you thought you knew was for sure and certain to realizing that everything is up for grabs. The empathetic man understands and says, 'That's okay, Barry.'"

"It's like back in the Christopher Columbus era—everyone believed that the world was flat. Now he's just sailed around the world to prove that it's in fact round."

"On Destiny's Highway you're working with love in following your destiny; that is, learning what love is by loving yourself and understanding you are a creator. What you feel determines your reality.

"Sometime, probably early in your life, you had to fit into your surroundings to survive. You had to do what the adults did and that's shut your feelings away. The innocent child is powerless, everything comes from outside of yourself, food does, shelter does and love does. But to get those things, you have to toe the line and do what you're told. The coper sees that things are outside of himself, so he has to figure out what the lay of the land is and then he steps in and takes over. The coper sees that love comes from outside of yourself and you have to do things to get it. The coper works out what do you have to do to survive and maybe get whatever crumbs of love that may come your way.

"Whereas now, empathetic Barry embraces the boy and generates love for himself. The main thing is that he doesn't have to do anything. It's totally unconditional, not what he thinks is love, usually fear dressed up as love. He embraces him at the worst times and says, 'It doesn't matter.' That's what love is, totally unconditional. That is what you are giving yourself, that's what you are generating yourself. That's how you learn what love really is. That's warmth you feel inside yourself when you empathize with the sadness.

"So off you went learning about ships and business, starting companies and gaining all these skills in man-made reality where we're taught that love is outside of yourself, where you're trying not to feel, because any feelings are looked upon as weakness. But love decrees that you will feel. So when you feel, you can empathize to generate warmth, and that's how you love yourself.

"The bottom line is within the universal limits—what you feel determines your reality.

"Feel what the boy feels—misery. Today is the same—misery. No matter how many times you've achieved success, there have been a few crumbs of fun, but they don't last. They go away, and then you're back to feeling miserable. To solve that, the coping part says go and make more money. Go and get a new car, a new woman, more money. You've dug 5000 tons of dirt and only got a few specks of gold. You're living in Struggleville, modern living but still in a fear-based reality, looking for a few carrots to relieve the feelings of misery.

"Which part of you is the strongest? Which part of you are you constantly trying to get away from, to try and overcome? Answer? The miserable feeling, the unworthiness.

"Which one has the most strength? The unworthiness has. The black has. What if you had that strength work for you? That's what you have just started to do—that's what this is about.

"Let's feel what the boy feels now and see how your reality has created the same thing over and over again in the women that have come into your life.

"The boy feels unworthy. Love comes from outside of yourself. Women are bad news, they hurt you. From then on it has been the same. Different people, different women, different scenes, different places but the same energy, the same feeling. Would that be correct, Barry?"

"Yes," Barry said.

"That's the magic. It happens every day. What you feel determines your reality. Everyone is the same. All our energies are determining Struggleville in reality, and it is right in front of our face every day to show us how we feel—to show us how much power we have.

"Think of it like an iceberg. You can only see the part above the water. The vast majority (90%) is underwater. If the current is taking it south and you want to go north, standing on top with oars and trying to row yourself north won't help. You'll still go south. The current is too strong and the majority of the iceberg is in the current.

"Your feelings are too strong. The love agenda is working regardless of what you're thinking and what you think you want. You think you must be going north because you've been paddling so hard and for so long. You have exhausted so much energy, but if you stop and look up, you would see that in fact you are drifting south, and always have been no matter how hard and fast you've been paddling. The only landmark that can tell you where you really are is your feelings. If you're not happy 24/7 and you feel unworthy, you're paddling north but drifting south. That's how it is and that's all we've known since time began. Now it's time for us to work with love, to live with the love agenda.

"Everyone has flaws and everyone has fears. Everyone has some combination of physical, mental and/or relationship problems. Whatever's not at ease within creates disease without to show you that you're not feeling happy within. These are the alarms—flashing lights on the outside to tell you things aren't happy inside. If you're disconnected from your feelings, they'll determine your reality again and again right in front of your face until you see that they determine your reality.

"Everyone has blind spots that they can't see about themselves. You might be able to see their hang-ups, but you might not be able to see your own. It's time to acknowledge these blind spots, embrace them, and use them for our learning. We need to look at our feelings in a new light and see them as the only real thing we have. The only things that are real are the things that last. The only things that last are our feelings.

"What we do is work with the iceberg. We work with the love agenda, we convert the energy to worthiness and then things can be different. You're ready for the next stage when you get to it—changing reality. Are you with me, Barry?"

"Pretty much got it. But what should I do? I was going to go away for a while, go on a cruise or travel or something."

"The innocent boy is still going to be there no matter where you go and what you do. Remember that what you feel determines what you create, so that applies wherever and whatever. People will look outside to change feelings. This may work for a short time, but it won't last. People will travel all over the place searching for themselves. The only place they don't go is back to themselves, to where the child lives.

"People spend a lot of time and money on things outside themselves. They've analyzed themselves upside down, they have gone to therapists who've analyzed them upside down. They've done a thousand and one coping techniques. Still the child is down the hole, and nothing is going to change until they begin the process of empathy; that is, get on Destiny's Highway and work with love's agenda.

"The most important thing is to begin the empathy that you've just begun. After all, the child has felt so miserable for such a long time, he deserves your attention. He has to be put first on the list, don't you think?"

"Fair enough, I agree."

"So what do you wish to do?"

"I think I'll stick around and come back and see you for a while. How often do you want to see me?"

"It's a process. I'm here to help you stay connected with yourself and learn how the judger controls you all the time to prevent you from being empathetic. The opposite of empathy is judgment, so look at it as a challenge between the two. The judger has been running the show. Today, empathy has just begun. It's your choice where you want to put your energy. For homework, we need to use a method that will allow you to stay aware of the boy, because your day-to-day dealings will take you away from him.

"People often get the process and it's reinforced while they're seeing me. However, it might be months or years later before empathy gains ground in some areas. One method is to find some photos of you and go and spend some time with yourself to remember and feel what it was like then so the connection stays strong."

"I don't have anything. We couldn't afford photos."

"Can you still see the boy now?"

Barry stared off into space, a look of concentration in his eyes.

"Close your eyes if you like," Michael said.

When he closed his eyes, Barry soon found him again. "Yeah I've got him, still with me."

"Good. You see, just by you talking to me you lost track of him. It doesn't take much initially to lose him. The empathetic man is pro-active. He tries to reach him and does things to hang onto him. Why not set your mobile phone to beep at you every hour? That's the boy ringing you up to make sure you're on the empathetic channel.

"Every night talk to him and say, 'Is there anything you want to show me tonight while I'm asleep to help us get closer together?' That way you're acknowledging him and valuing him and reaching out to him—giving him permission to be with you.

"If you have any songs or movies that move you or make you feel sad, then go and watch them. The more you feel, the more you can connect with him. Remember, sadness is warmth. I know that what I'm laying out seems totally illogical, but bear with me.

"Let's say you're in deep water and the only thing you have on your mind is to keep your head above the surface by treading water. When I'm asking you to feel sad, it's like asking you to let go, to stop treading water. The logical coper will do anything to keep his head above the water, to keep breathing air. It will tread water the best it can. No matter how hard and fast you tread water you can't get out of the water.

"What I'm asking you is to stop treading water and let go. By switching to empathy and feeling the sadness, you think you'll drown. That's logic talking. But what you did today—converting sadness to warmth—was to show you that you won't drown. When you do that process 100 out of 100 times, you'll find that sadness is warmth every time. When you've done it enough, I won't have to keep telling you, you'll understand that. It's like you develop gills and gain the ability to breathe underwater. If you let go and go one foot under water, you didn't drown. Your logic meanwhile will try and keep your head above water and bring you back. You'll bob up and down many times; you'll switch from one to the other over and over again until the empathy becomes strong enough to run the Barry Corporation. Then you'll be able to let go deeper and deeper and still be able to breathe. So the deeper you sink, the blacker it gets, and the warmer it gets.

"When you're ready, you can deliberately remember the things that you have chosen to block out and feel them with empathy knowing that sadness is warmth and you'll be able to generate warmth from those times instead of blocking them, which would cause disease and struggle in your life.

"I'll write those things down for you if you like." Michael reached for a piece of paper.

"Sure. What were they? To talk to the boy at night?" Barry tried to remember.

"Yes, and ask if there's anything he wants to show you while you're asleep to help you two get closer together. Also, photos, if any, songs and movies to stir you up to get the sadness going for generating warmth. When you're reading, you'll start to remember things in life which you have deliberately blocked off—the ones that you feel the most. Set your phone so the boy can remind you to be with him."

"Good I'll make an appointment for next week."

"Okay. Let the adventure begin," replied Michael.

Chapter 8

Fred couldn't find a replacement for Schofields. The word around the industry was that Fred was going broke and anyone would have to be mad to work for him. One of his best salesmen was assigned to the manager's position at Fred's demand. He was a good salesman, but a terrible manager. The worse things got, the more Fred drank. He stayed away from home more and found comfort in being with Pam, who was starting to have doubts about the wisdom of being in a relationship with her boss, especially one who soon might not even have a business to be boss of.

The head teacher at Brad's school had not heard from Mr. or Mrs. Murray, so she asked the school secretary to get Brad's contact details out of the filing cabinet. The first contact was Rosa's cell phone number. Upon calling the number, the call went to the message bank. She dialed the second contact—Fred's work number. The phone rang at Fred's work. Pam let him know that it was Brad's school on the line.

"Hello, Fred Murray here." Fred spoke in his best voice. He was anxious to know the reason why he was talking to the school. Even though he didn't know it, his "little boy" from his school days was trying to tell him something. Fred had had some interactions with his teachers when he was a boy and that feeling of getting caught doing something wrong was never far from his mind whenever he was confronted by authority.

"Yes, Mr. Murray, it's Mrs. Doyle here. I'm Brad's head teacher. Did you receive our letter regarding Brad's school performance?"

"No I didn't," replied Fred, surprised.

"Well, we sent home a letter with Brad asking you to make an appointment to see me. We wish to discuss Brad's school performance. He's falling behind in a number of areas."

"Look, Mrs. Doyle, my wife usually looks after that sort of thing. I'll look into it and call you back tomorrow." Fred was embarrassed.

"Thank you, Mr. Murray, it's in Brad's best interests," she assured him.

"Of course. Thank you for the call."

Fred actually went home on time to get to the bottom of what was happening with Brad. He was fired up with a few beers under his belt, so he was ready by the time Rosa had arrived home with Brad from basketball again.

As soon as they came through the door Fred yelled out, "Brad, get in here!"

Brad felt sick in the stomach because he knew by the sound of his father's voice that he was in for it.

"I got a phone call today, and guess who it was from?"

"Who?"

"Mrs. Doyle. You know her, do you?"

"Oh," said Brad as he put his head down.

"Oh, shit," said Rosa.

Fred was on a roll. "As if it isn't enough that you're nothing but a slacker, you don't give us notes from school to tell us that you're a slacker. You're nothing but a waste of time, boy!"

"But, Dad I did," Brad said softly. He knew from past experience that he couldn't say anything to his dad that was going to make a scrap of difference when he was in that state.

"You've been nothing but trouble since the day you were

born. I can't be bothered with wasting my money on sending you to school, why should I bother sending you to school?" Fred yelled out.

Rosa stepped in "Stop it! He did give me the note. I left it in the car and forgot all about it."

"You did? You're just as hopeless as he is. You're pathetic. Seeing as you two have messed everything up, I'll leave it to you to sort it out. She, whatever her name is, Mrs. Boyle or whatever, wants to hear from me tomorrow, so you two can tell her what's happening; you two can sort it—I'm going to the club."

Yes, that will certainly help the situation, Rosa thought to herself, staring at Fred contemptuously.

"What's that look for? You solve it; it's your doing. Call her tomorrow and sort it!" Fred yelled as he walked out the door.

Brad retreated to his room and pulled out the guitar from under his bed and started to strum it.

Rosa got a drink, pulled herself together, and walked into Brad's room. "Where did you get that? Did you steal it?"

"Mom!" Brad said, hurt that his mother would think that of him. "Shane lent it to me for music at school. I have to practice songs."

"Don't let your father catch you; he forbids you from playing music. You know he thinks it's a waste of time."

"Yeah, I don't care what he says. He's an idiot."

Just then, Sarah interrupted them as she came through the back door, "Are you ready, Rosa?"

"Oh, shit, I have to play basketball. We'll talk when I get home," she said to Brad.

Brad didn't answer because he didn't care one way or the other.

"Hi Sarah. I won't be long," Rosa called out as she went into her bedroom.

Sarah saw Deb come out of her room and asked her, "How did you do on the math exam? Lyn got her results today; she did really well."

Destiny's Highway

"Yeah, I know, she did better than me."

"Really? That's a surpise," said Sarah

"What's a surprise?" asked Rosa.

"Lyn beat Deb in a math test."

Rosa looked at Deb as if to say "what's happening to you?" The look was enough for Deb to feel bad.

"Let's go and kick some butt, Rosa. Bye, Deb."

"Bye," said Deb as she walked into Brad's room. "What was Dad going on about before?"

"Same old, same old—you know—I'm hopeless and a waste of space and blah, blah, blah."

"He's always picked on you. He treats me different from you; I'm his favorite. It's not fair to you. Thank goodness he doesn't treat me like you—I don't think I could handle it."

"How about that—Lyn beat Deb in a math exam," continued Sarah in the car with Rosa.

Rosa just looked across at Sarah.

"That Michael stuff is doing her some good. You know, I'm going to see him as well and so is James.

"Is that right?" Rosa said.

"Yes, I put Lyn's improvement in the math exam down to the methods that Michael showed her."

"Maybe he could help Brad. We got a letter from the school about him. I lost it and the school called Fred."

"Woo! I bet that didn't go down too well."

"No, he of course ripped into Brad and then me. And then went to the pub as usual. Whenever any problems come up he disappears and blames it on me if things go wrong."

"Give Michael a call; I'll give you his card."

"Thanks."

Chapter 9

"Hello, Lyn and Sarah," said Michael.

"Hello, Michael. I'm leaving Lyn with you and I'll be back with James; we're next."

"Sure thing. I'll see you later."

"How are you doing?"

"Great—I got 85% on my math test! Usually I have trouble passing."

'Well, I can see you've been empathetic to yourself."

"The best I can, but the judger is still there."

"At this stage it'll always be trying to block you off or hassle you. So you must be pleased with yourself?"

"I am, I am."

"So let's keep it going!

"What we'd like to do today is get a little closer to the feeling part and go down and meet it. The way we do that is to relax or to help you to go within you. What I like to do is for you to sit in this relaxation chair so you can let go and relax. It's like a set of steps. Step 1 is awake, then it goes down to step 100 and that's asleep.

"In the middle we're aware of both our outer worlds—our thinking part—and at the same time our inner world—the feeling part—where all the feeling Lyns live. I relax you down so the empathetic Lyn can listen to the feeling Lyns easier. You'll be aware of this room and me and at the same time you'll be aware of what's coming from within you.

"There's nothing happening out here to grab your attention, just me, you and a room. That allows you to focus on the Lyns within that in itself says to them 'You are important. I want to get to know you and I want to rescue you, wherever you are and whatever has happened to you.' You don't have to try and do anything, just let go. Then, just drift and let come whatever comes whether it's feelings, memories, body sensations, anything. Just listen to her feelings, they are her language, and empathize with whatever the Lyns want to show you."

Lyn sat in the big leather reclining chair and started to laugh.

"What's happening?" asked Michael

"I've just watched too many movies, that's all. Shrink's chair and all that."

"Let yourself laugh and when you're finished, let me know. Let it out of your system, remember the same applies to any other feelings—crying, breathing, your body might start twitching, and laughing, so treat your body as a friend. After all, it's the bottle. Let it feel what it wants to feel."

Lyn relaxed easily and started to see all the Lyns that she had already met—the pre-school one, the primary school one, and the exam one.

They were still there feeling safe. Michael had expected it. Lyn surely had done some homework and had gotten a result already.

"Is there any Lyn that wants to show you anything, any Lyn that wants to tell you something?"

"I'm at the pre-school again."

"How's she feeling?"

"She's in the bathroom hiding from the kids." Her tears started again.

"Ask empathetic Lyn to come in again?"

"Yes, she's here."

"What's happening with the little girl?"

"She's so shattered," she said, starting to cry.

"Yes, she is. You know, the thing is Lyn, most people have no idea how sad they are. At this stage you can think of it as a black coal mine—the more you dig, the more you convert to electricity. You keep doing it until all the coal has been converted, then the next phase begins."

"Billy Adams was nothing but an idiot! How can such a loser laughing at me shatter me so badly? He should not affect me so much; I'm better than that. I'm better than him." After a little while she said, "He wouldn't let me go, he followed me when I wanted to run away, I started crying, and he followed me all around the playground until I had to hide in the bathroom to get away from him." Another wave of sadness. "If this is the problem, that Billy's a bastard, then I've been hiding ever since. All the problems with exams and singing. My teacher thinks that I could go somewhere with my singing, but I haven't been able to do it. I hate Billy Adams, he makes me so angry! He's messed my life up! But I'm not like that. I don't hate anyone and I'm not an angry person!" exclaimed Lyn.

"Can you see how the judger comes in?" Michael asked. "Just let yourself feel, be with the little girl and just let her feel what she wants to feel without all the comments, the analysis and the censorship. So what. Where does that leave the girl? Still trapped in the bathroom feeling hopeless, sad and alone. All the judger does is stop you from empathizing with her."

Crying, sighing and with her body starting to twitch, Lyn spent some time letting go, then she said, "I feel peaceful—drained, but good." With that she opened her eyes.

"Let's see if I can put a different slant on Billy for you. To love yourself, you need to feel what love isn't. You see, love doesn't waste any energy. All your experiences have been designed for one thing –for you to learn to love yourself. Not one experience has been wasted. Every detail is there waiting for you to turn it to warmth. Nothing has been a waste of time. It's like black coal, stored away for a time when the empathetic Lyn can go there and dig it out and convert it to warmth. All roads lead to Rome. Black is white and they're all designed to love you. That's how you love yourself.

"Billy has helped you make coal. He's played a big part in the play that you designed for yourself so you could feel what it feels like to feel unworthiness, fear, sadness, and loneliness. Now it's time for you to convert the unworthiness to worthiness by generating the warmth from the black—well, what we think of as black, anyhow. Do you understand?"

Lyn nodded her head.

"Very good. Now you can continue to carry out this process if you like at home as often as you wish. Same as before, but spend some quiet time with yourself as well and relax down and tune into yourself and see what happens. Let the empathy get stronger. Well, I think your mom and dad are next to come in. What's happening to you?"

"I'm going to sit in the car and read my novel," said Lyn.

"Okay, I'll see you next time."

"Bye, and thank you so much."

"My pleasure!"

Chapter 10

Sarah and James exchanged greetings with Lyn, who was pleased to see her parents. After sitting down and getting their details, Michael asked, "How can I help?"

Sarah looked at James and James looked at Sarah and they both smiled.

"Well, I'll start," said James. "I've come to the point where I think I've got a problem. I get scared and jealous when Sarah wants to go out somewhere. I get angry. I think she's having an affair. The other night I got so wild up I went out and smashed her car window so she couldn't go out. I lose it, but after I calm down I'm really sorry and fully intend not to do it again, but it happens again.

"It's getting worse and what happened the other night is not good for Lyn, Sarah, or my bank account. It's bad for me, too. I've never hit Sarah or Lyn, but I take it out on the furniture or other things. I've punched many a wall. I've put my fist through doors and walls lots of times, even before I got married. It's like I'd rather hurt myself than any of my family and friends.

"We went to another marriage guidance lady before and I felt that she blamed me for our problems and told me to get some anger management. She told me not to dominate and smother my wife and to get off her back." James had finished his bit and looked at Sarah who joined in.

Destiny's Highway

"I've never given him any reason not to trust me. I deliberately don't go out most of the time because it's not worth the hassle. James is a good husband in many other ways, but I think that he's extremely insecure, probably because of his upbringing. His mother and father always used to fight and both had affairs. But it's wearing me down. Why should I not have a life just because he can't handle it? I could be out having a career, but I can't because he doesn't want me to be out there. He thinks I'm going to run off with somebody.

"I do want him to be my husband, but I want to be me. I didn't mind raising Lyn, but I don't want to be trapped at home and just kill time. Life is too short. Many times I thought of leaving, but he's a good man and I do love him, but what can you do? I know I'm not perfect, but I can't do this anymore—I'm at my wit's end."

"Fair enough," Michael said. "Remember what I was telling Lyn?" he said as he looked at Sarah. She nodded her head. "Let's show James and refresh it for you at the same time and then I'll apply it to relationships." After explaining about the different parts to James and about how empathy works, Michael went on.

"Let me draw it for you.

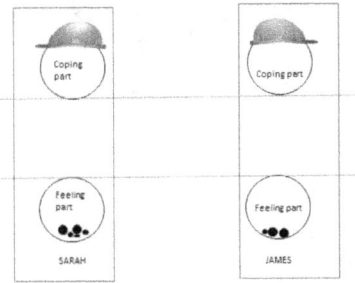

"There is Sarah—her adult and her child, her thinking part and her feeling part and here is James, two parts just like Sarah.

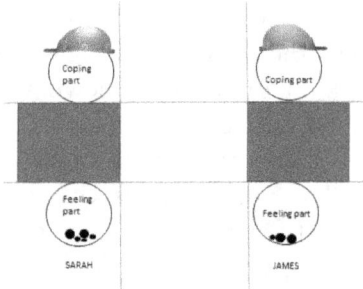

"Like everyone else, there's a gap between the two; they're not connected with themselves.

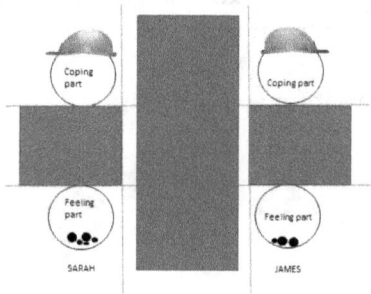

"When you got married, Sarah didn't know who Sarah really was and James didn't know who James really was. Both of you were split—there's no connection between your two parts.

Destiny's Highway

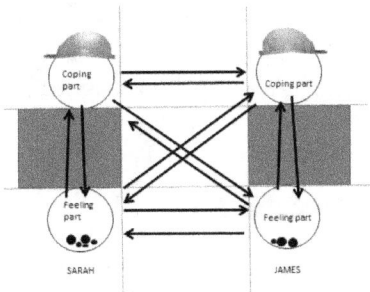

"In this situation, there are many lines of communication that can play a role in the relationship and they can switch back and forth at any time it seems.

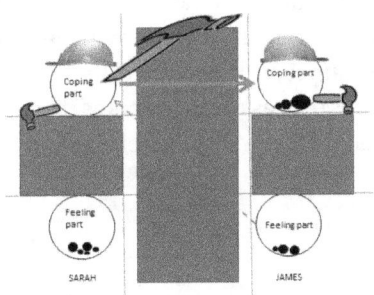

"So love, your feelings and your innocence, wants to get the coping, logical adult's attention, so both feelings parts use the opposite adult to treat their adult partner in the same way as the adult treats the child inside of themselves.

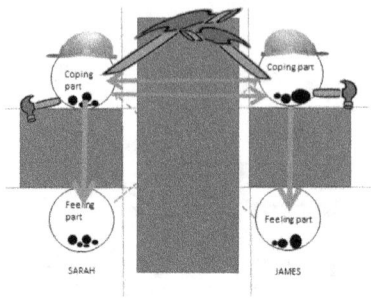

"You don't listen to the child, you don't want to feel the child. You block them off. You don't love the child, so it gets your partner to treat you, the adult, in the same way as you treat the child. The adult is looking for love outside of itself—looking for love from the other partner to try and fulfil the emptiness inside. No matter what your partner does, they'll not be able to fill that emptiness. Big Sarah cannot make little James happy and little Sarah cannot be made happy by whatever James does. Looking for love outside of you is futile. So Sarah, no matter how many times you try and stay home to please James, it'll never work.

"Again, it's a process and it takes time, but gradually empathy will reign after many switches of governance within self.

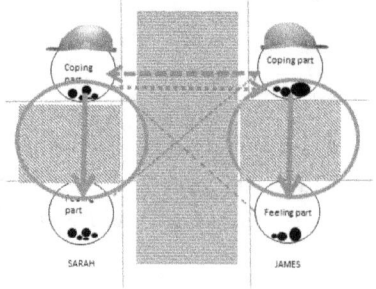

Destiny's Highway

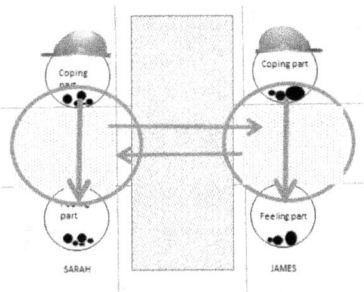

"The battle between judgment and empathy continues until both individuals become whole.

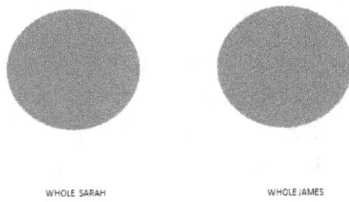

"We're here now to help Sarah connect with innocent Sarah so Sarah is complete and I'm here to help James connect with little James so James can find out who James is. I'm here to help you have a relationship with yourself first.

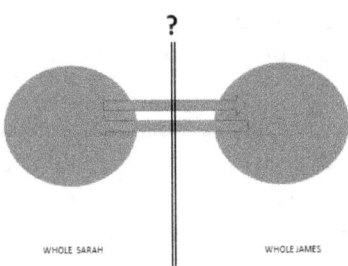

"Then you can decide if you want to have a relationship with each other. Then you'll have two people in the relationship rather than four modes that you have now, i.e., child Sarah, adult Sarah, child James, and adult James. You two can switch modes from day to day, hour to hour, and minute to minute, so a conversation can be taking place between four different modes in the space of a minute.

"How could anyone possibly resolve anything like that? It just makes you feel more confused and mixed up. When this happens, the innocent child says, 'Perfect! That's exactly what I want you to feel,' so you can experience what the child in each of you is experiencing, feel it, empathize with it, and generate your own warmth from it. The universe has designed it so that your partner is there to treat you the same way as you treat yourself. If it's unworthy, then it's to show you that a part of you is feeling unworthy. You fluctuate in your treatment of yourself. So, too, your partner will fluctuate in their treatment of you accordingly.

"What we're after is empathetic James being with empathetic Sarah. It always starts with yourself first. I work with Sarah and I work with James, then down the track we can come together, if you want to, as we go along. You will see that empathetic James wants to be with empathetic Sarah and vice versa. You can be free to be yourself and be with your partner. Right now, you don't know who you are, and empathy says that's okay.

"So, let empathy run the show, and see where it goes from there. Do you understand and do you want to proceed?"

"I do, for sure," Sarah said

"I want to save my marriage. I'll do it for you, Sarah," James replied.

"Not good enough, says innocent James," Michael said. "James, you want to do it for yourself. You see, innocent James has no one else. He's here to rescue you and you're here to rescue him. Can you see innocent James, now? Just take a moment and sense him."

"All I can see is a photo I have at home. It was a soccer photo they took before one of our games when I was about ten. I remember falling over and getting my white pants dirty before the photo," James recalled smiling. "They had to put me at the back so you couldn't see the dirt in the photo, and Dad and Mom were grabbing me and yelling at me in front of my friends." The smile disappeared and tears started to appear in his eyes.

"What's he feeling, James? Go down and be with him."

"He's so embarrassed and alone—he feels so alone!" Tears started to run down his face. "He's smiling in the photo, but he's crying on the inside.

That's about the only time my parents came to watch me play. They used to drop me off and pick me up after the game was over, but they were always late. I used to sit there for up to an hour sometimes wondering if they had forgotten me. The guys in the club used to look after me mostly," recalled James.

"Tell me, James, is this something you often do? I noticed when you were telling me about punching walls in, you were smiling. When you're talking about getting your pants dirty, you were smiling. Is that funny? Is that funny what's happening to the man that's punching the wall? Is he happy? Is that funny what's happening to the boy? Go down on the ground with him. Is it funny? See how Mr. Coper smiles to cover up the feelings to survive? It's like—don't show the enemy that you're hurting," stated Michael.

"No, it definitely is not funny. It's dead set sad," James replied.

"So feeling how sad he is, doesn't he demand your attention? He wants you to do it for you, doesn't he?"

"Yes. I want to do it for him—for me," James concluded.

"Do you see how futile it is to try and solve that feeling of being unloved? No matter what Sarah does, it's still going to be there. The only way to solve it is to turn it to warmth. What has happened by Sarah trying to solve the problem for you? It's driven her away from you and that makes you feel more insecure, which makes you react more. It's like you grabbing hold of her by the throat and yelling, 'Why don't you love me?' metaphorically speaking.

"As for you, Sarah, why have you sacrificed your social life and career?"

"To save my marriage," replied Sarah. "But I feel selfish saying this. I always feel guilty for saying what I want, so I just put up with it, but I hate it!"

"Let's have a listen to innocent Sarah. Can you sense her?"

"I'm with my father in his garage. I'm only little. I want to help him, but he tells me to go away. I tripped over and spilt some oil on the cement." Sarah paused.

"He yelled at me and I cried." Her eyes filled with tears. "All I wanted was attention and he yelled at me. He picked me up and put me inside the house and yelled at me 'to do as I was told for once!' It's been the same ever since. He makes me feel that whatever I do isn't good enough and whatever I say is stupid and what I want to do is of no value and no one takes any notice of me."

"Whatever you just said, Sarah, the girl is saying to you. She's telling you, 'You don't feel me so you don't listen to me, so you don't think I'm worth anything, I'm of no value to you.' This applies to your relationship with yourself and hence the innocent child has made you feel that with James. You're trying to get love and attention off James, but the girl won't let you; she's making you feel the same as she's feeling with James' help and vice versa. Whatever you do is not good enough and never will be. Do you see that?" Michael said

'Yes, that's unreal!" Sarah exclaimed, "I've been trying ever since I can remember. For the sixteen years of marriage, for sure."

"James, can you see that by trying to cope with your insecure feelings that eventually you would have driven Sarah away and she'd get sick of you trying to hold her back and smothering her? She'd eventually do exactly what your insecurity was telling you—she'd leave you and go with someone else. Then the insecurity would turn around and say, 'See, I told you so. You can't trust people and they only leave you,' proving what you feel you create.

"That's why today this is a special time. This is the first time in your life where you've generated love for yourself. How special is that? It's the start, it's begun and you won't want to do anything else because it feels so good. There'll be stages when you think you're going backwards, but that'll be the judger coming in to test you. It'll find any cracks in your system where you don't love yourself and after a while it'll help you see them because you'll feel the difference. Empathy is warm, mellow, gentle, and fresh, whereas judgment feels thick, stale, sick, and dull. Like you are dragging your ass, basically.

"There'll be times when you think it's too hard. There'll be many fluctuations, but at this stage you must always go back to the child to get the sad, warm, mellow feeling—the feeling of being connected with yourself," Michael concluded.

"Well, you've certainly given us something to work with. You know, I wasn't that keen on coming after being judged last time by that other lady. And I was just coming along because Sarah and Lyn wanted me to. I didn't expect much after last time, but now I'm in for sure. I'll give it a go. I'll do my best, and as a result, it'll hopefully help our relationship and our family. I have a good feeling about this; I think that this could work. What do you think, Sarah?" James turned to Sarah.

"I'm looking forward to it," said Sarah.

"I'll say again, there'll be challenges and there'll be times when you wish you didn't start, but that's the judgment creeping in. As you go along, though, I know a few things about the judgment, so I'm sure you'll be all right." Michael concluded the session.

"I think we should go out for dinner. What do you reckon, Sarah?" James felt uplifted.

"That would be lovely." Sarah left the room with a smile on her dial.

Chapter 11

Rosa managed to get an appointment for Brad. She didn't want to wait any longer to get Brad the help that she thought he needed.

"Hello. Brad is it?" asked Michael.

"Yes, that's me," replied Brad.

"Come on in and take a seat, Brad. Let me take a few details and we'll have a chat." Michael noticed a shy young man, but he had a spark in his eye. "What brings you here?" Michael asked.

"Mom reckons I have a bad attitude towards school, and Dad thinks I'm a waste of space."

"What do you reckon?" Michael returned.

"I reckon Dad's never home, he puts shit on Mom, and Mom tries to do everything because Dad's not there. She can't manage, but puts up with it. I think Dad is an asshole and the teachers suck. I don't see what they go on about. I'm just about finished. This year is my last, so what's the point."

"Is there anything you like about your life?"

"I like music. I like playing guitar, and I like to sing. I'm no good at organized sports, and I like to play video games. I like surfing." Brad looked away wondering where Michael was going with all this.

"Let me tell you a few things and let's see how they sit with you."

Destiny's Highway

"Okay," he replied.

"When you're a kid you have no say and you have no choice. Big people tell you where to go and what to do and if you don't do it, then there are consequences. They mean well most of the time, but their well-meaning is lost in translation. If someone is pushing you, you either do as you're told or resist. You're too small to beat them, so you can fight as much as you like, but you can't win.

"What if you're caught in a riptide in the surf? If you try and swim against it, you'll drown; if you go with it, you'll end up out to sea and drown anyway. The way you get out is swim across it. What I'm offering you are ways to swim across the rip in your life because at the moment you are drowning.

"You're fighting against it. You're not doing your schoolwork, you hate your teachers, you hate your dad—they're controlling your life, even though you're resisting them because they have power over you. You then give up and go into your room, go into another reality. You play video games, but you can't stay there forever, eventually you have to face reality. There seems only two ways. One is to say that life sucks and accept it, give up, and judge yourself forever. That isn't the only way, though. Love has a plan for you, and we call it Destiny's Highway. Are you interested in traveling Destiny's Highway, Brad?"

Brad had been listening intently. He somehow understood and felt safe. "Sure, I'm listening. What's next?"

"Just go with me, Brad. How far back can you remember yourself?"

During the session, something clicked inside of Brad. Brad felt for the first time in his life he was empowered to be himself. He was determined to run his own race and use the so-called coal inside of him to generate his power to be himself. By the end of the session, he was quite strong and looked forward to running his own race to show himself what he could do for himself. He was starting to see his father as a frightened little boy who acted out and used power to get people before they got him. He could see that his parents were trying to do the right thing by him. He didn't like the pressure and the hassles, but could now start to use them for his own growth.

He was now going to try and start to determine his own life and not be a victim anymore. He used to use "woe is me" as a way to cope. He'd switch back and forth, but he had a direction now—something to work with and he was going to give it his best shot. He was intelligent, but refrained from showing it to piss his dad off. In his father's eyes he was nothing. He realized that by believing his father he'd eventually end up exactly where his father said he would be—nowhere.

"How did he do?" asked Rosa as she arrived to pick him up. "What did you talk about?"

"Brad can fill you in if he wants to," answered Michael. "He did well, he understands what to do, and it's up to him, now. I'll see you next time, Brad."

As soon as Brad got in the car, he gave Rosa a hug. "Thanks for everything you've done for me. I'm sorry for messing you around. I intend to change from now on and I know how to do it, now. I'm not saying it's going to happen overnight, but it'll happen. By the way, you and Dad have to come to the presentation night at the end of the year. I have a surprise for you and yes I'll remind you and Dad when it's on."

"What do you mean, remind me? I don't need to be reminded," she joked.

"No, of course not, Mom. I'll just write it on a note and give it to you."

"Shut up, you smart alec." Rosa drove out onto the road.

"You know those music records that Dad has in your wardrobe? Are they still there?"

"Yes, I think so. They're all the favorite records your father used to have when he was young. Isn't that funny, I just remembered that his father forbade Fred from playing records at his home. They were strict religious people and forbid records. So he used to buy them and play them over at my house, and he kept them there. Why do you ask?"

"I was just thinking."

When they got home Fred was nowhere to be seen. "Has your father come home yet, Deb?" called out Rosa.

"No I haven't seen or heard from him."

"I'll get dinner ready," Rosa said as she pulled out some frozen fish and put it in the microwave.

"Mom, do you mind if I look in the bottom of your wardrobe at those records of Dad's?" Brad asked.

"No, I'll come with you." There must have been about thirty records in the bottom of the wardrobe. They were mainly of two artists.

"They must have been his favorites. They used to wear long hair, like hippies in Forrest Gump." Brad started to turn over the covers and read the words of the songs. Rosa left him to it.

Fred arrived home when everyone else in the house was asleep. Once again, he slept on the lounge.

The next morning Brad was on a mission. He was up, ready on time, and stirring up his sister.

"Dopey," he said as he went into the bathroom as Deb was brushing her teeth. "Do you have any friends that work in a music shop?"

"Yes. Lyn does on the weekend; her singing teacher got the job for her," mumbled Deb with a mouth full of toothpaste.

"I'm coming over to her place with you, I want to ask her something. Hurry up, let's go!"

"I'm going over to Lyn's place with Deb, Mom. I'll catch the bus to the station, I'll have plenty of time."

"Brad, tell your Mrs. Doyle that we've sorted something out and I'll call her if she wishes." Rosa kissed her kids good-bye.

Brad and Lyn sat together on the bus. They were in a deep discussion about something, but Deb was too busy looking cool for a boy that she liked to be bothered with Brad's capers.

Chapter 12

As the weeks rolled by, the Bookers came and learned more about how their sense of unworthiness was affecting their marriage.

James could see how insecure he felt about himself no matter what Sarah did. It's like he had a pair of glasses on and no matter how or what or who he looked at, he was still feeling insecure. He truly understood how strong his feelings were.

Sarah had felt it was the right thing to do to stay home so her husband would not feel his insecurity. She did it for sixteen years and it hadn't worked. All that happened was she got drained and resentful while James' insecurity got worse. Sarah became drained and James didn't learn anything. Sarah didn't learn anything because she assumed that helping someone like that was the right thing to do.

Besides, trying to help James took her mind off herself. In every case, trying to help someone at your own cost will not help them or you in the long run. In fact, Michael suggested that this common belief was the biggest trick of the coping world. How noble is it that you help someone and support them, help them cope with their sadness, fear, and loneliness. When in fact, from a Love perspective, you're delaying the inevitable; that is, the fact is that you will suffer until you feel things enough to put yourself on the list and love yourself.

If we understood the magnitude of a person's soul and the depth of their feelings, we'd understand that anyone's help will have a limiting affect. Their feelings of futility will soon create a futile world for them and any help from anyone will be completely swamped by their futility, to the effect that they'll turn on the helper and smash them back. Until they realize their power, that they've created their world and they have free will to change themselves, 'help' from others is like giving them a bunch of flowers, reminding them there's something better, there's a god, there's love. When it's all said and done, only they can help themselves. That's what the deal is.

That's where empathy comes in, when you are empathetic to yourself you will help others, but not at your own cost and in a way that will really help them. Sometimes Love will let people suffer, after all the entire child is trying to use the suffering to get the adult to feel, so they will love themselves. If you, 'the helper', prevents this from happening, then you are working against the innocence and Love. You, the giver, gets drained (that's for you to learn) and the taker's suffering is eased (they don't feel it) and hence their innocence will do it again, only harder next time.

Barry also continued with his adventure. He could see that most of his life was focused on his businesses and trying to find the right woman. He worked tirelessly on both and began to see that all his energy was going away from him—it was time to spend time on himself.

He could see that despite all the energy he'd spent on trying to be happy from outside of himself he still felt lonely, sad and unworthy. It was the unworthiness that drove him to have more money than he knew what to do with. He just didn't stop; his logical coper kept on making money, because from its perspective that's what was going to solve the feeling of unworthiness. Barry could now see that it was a way to occupy his time so he wouldn't have time to really feel as bad as he was feeling. He did it to take his mind off himself because he didn't know what else to do. But now it wasn't working; he wasn't coping anymore.

"Good," said Michael. "Now you know coping doesn't work. From love's perspective, you're not here to cope, you're here to feel and to love yourself. You're here to see that you're a creator so you can fulfil your destiny, not just score points with the system that takes your energy and tells you to jump through hoops and how to feel. We try to create a virtual reality instead of being real—to feel. So we create a 'dead zone' and we live in it.

"We're not here to feed the stagnant pond system in the mountain stream analogy, but to let the life force, your feelings, flow through you to feel what love isn't so then you will convert it to what love is.

"Futility is being born in unworthiness and dying feeling unworthy, but having coped really well. The coping part falls away at death, because it's not real. The only thing that's real are things that last. Your soul lasts and feelings are your energy, your soul, the energy that creates things, the part of us that is part of the whole universe, that's what lasts."

As Barry progressed, he realized how powerful loneliness was inside of him. He'd rather be treated badly by his women than be lonely. He realized even when he was with someone he still felt alone. Coping wasn't helping, but the coping part is tricky in that it makes you think it is. As he embraced himself, the loneliness was disappearing and he felt quite contented with his own company. Now he embraced himself, walked around with it, and it changed to warmth.

The depth and strength of his loneliness was underestimated. Everyone is not aware of the depth and intensity of their unworthiness, loneliness, and abandoned feelings that they're trying to cope with. Once we have walked along the empathy track and have felt the intensity of the feelings, we realize how futile it is for the coper to get a result. It's like trying to change the course of a battle ship with a mosquito.

That's why it's a process; it takes as long as it takes. Of course, the coping part has been active for a long time—it hasn't gone away and he fluctuates between the two—but the empathy is certainly getting stronger. His usual way of solving his loneliness would be to go out and look for another girlfriend. But for now it was time to have a relationship with himself.

He realized that when you look for love outside—trying to score points with people or trying to live up to their expectations—you'll always end up being used and coming unglued in some way. Whenever you are jumping through hoops to look better in someone else's eyes, you're only proving to yourself that you feel unworthy and so what you feel is what you create.

Barry had experienced and seen the same patterns occurring again and again. He knew that he was doing the same thing and yet he couldn't stop it no matter how hard he tried. He used to use meditation, motivation, and positive affirmations. Nothing worked. He'd read many books on self-help. They all sounded good, but they didn't work. He often would get a brain snap trying to figure out why the stuff in the books didn't work; he thought he really must be screwed. He would go to seminars on motivation and self-help and he'd be pumped up for a few days, but eventually the same old same old feelings would come back.

Michael explained, "Let's say you have a rusty car and you take it to a body shop and you ask the guy to fix it up. The guy tells you he can, then he goes inside and matches up the paint. Then he comes out and sprays paint over the rust. Then he turns around and tells you it's fixed. Your reaction is, 'No way is it fixed!' and you probably won't be going to the body shop again. You'd take the car to a guy that will get the rust out first and then repaint it."

Barry had been around the traps; he had been to plenty of spray painters, but the rust still remained. He found that the empathy work was sustainable, lasting, and worked every time. He was removing the rust.

Chapter 13

Fred felt weak. He knew it was wrong to look for comfort in Pam's arms, but it was easy and she was available. He felt guilty for how he treated Rosa, but it was easier to not think about it and when he did think about it, it was easy to blame her for his troubles. After all, Rosa had failed him. She was supposed to take care of him, not the other way around. It was his job to make money and provide for his family. It was her job to make sure things ran smoothly at home and to take care of his emotional and physical needs. It had been a long time since she had been anything but a burden, and who could blame him for wanting to have his needs satisfied?

"Pam, could you come into my office, please?"

Pam brought in her notebook and sat down. "Yes, Mr. Murray?"

"Pam, this isn't about work; it's about us. I don't know what to say. I'm sorry for the trouble I've caused."

Pam nodded her head.

"I don't want to lose you, Pam. I love you and I need you, and I'm sorry I hurt you. Can you forgive me?"

Pam walked over and kissed him. "It's okay, Fred. I understand. Things are rough right now. I won't give up on you."

* * *

Destiny's Highway

Although Fred felt better about Pam, he was worried sick about business. There was never enough time in the day and with most of his energy going into handling the work that Schofields used to do, he didn't have enough time to take care of customers or seek out new business. He knew his business was going to fail if he didn't do something about it soon, but he didn't know how to even get started. With all the chaos in his personal life, he found it hard to focus. It was easier to do simple manager-related work instead of building relationships. It was hard to give when he was in such need himself.

If only his home life was working like it should. If Rosa would step up and take care of her responsibilities, he'd be able to focus on work and his business wouldn't be failing.

Fred's thoughts continued to circle between Rosa, Pam, and his business troubles. He opened his bottom desk drawer and poured himself a drink. There was always one sure way to stop his racing thoughts. He called Pam back into his office.

* * *

Barry was en route to a function that approached Fred's office block. He had some time to spare, so thought he would pop in on Fred.

As Barry was about to enter Fred's office, he could see Fred and Pam embracing in Fred's room. He called out to save any embarrassment. "Fred, are you there? It's Barry." Coming out of his room, red-faced, Fred didn't know what to say. Pam soon followed, said hello to Barry, and shot through.

"What's happening, Fred?" asked Barry.

"I see that you're back on deck. How's it going? Sort things out?" Fred tried to change the subject.

"I'm great, thanks, but how about you?"

"Fine, things are fine."

"Bullshit, Fred. I've known you for how long? We went to business school together before you were married. So if things are going so well, how come you're cuddling your secretary? And you look like shit, by the way. Listen Fred, you haven't got many real people in your life and until recently, neither had I. You know those people that pat you on the back, but at the same time punch you in the gut? We have plenty of them to deal with in our line of work. But I'm genuine, my friend. I'd like to give you a reality check and I do it as a friend. I've got to tell you, Schofields left you because his assessment was that your strategy to survive in business was severely flawed. I'm telling you this as a true friend, Fred."

Fred nodded his head and listened.

"I've tried to help you. I stepped back so you could stand on your own feet, but there are times when you have to take a look at yourself. That's what I've just done and I'll tell you it's the best thing I could have done. I should have done it earlier, but my ego got in the way. Fred, don't you think there's a problem when you're cuddling your secretary and you look like an alcoholic? It's not a good look having beer cans on your desk. How many cigarettes are you smoking?

"Anyway, what about Brad and Deb? They're great kids. I'm no expert my friend, but you're going to end up a poor old man with a bottle in his hand in the park and no one around you.

"One thing I've learned is that you won't find happiness in another woman's arms until you find happiness inside yourself; on that I am an expert. My friend, I think it's time for you to reassess things. If you want, I can give you some pointers, so give us a call. I'm back feeling a lot better and a lot wiser. Catch you later, I better go."

Fred looked at Barry as he walked away. He felt something shift inside of him, but he pushed it away. What did Barry know, anyway? He had it easy. He had a lot of money and was successful at almost everything. Not relationships, of course, but who cared about relationships when you had that much money? Fred shook his head, gathered his things, and headed for the bus stop.

Chapter 14

Fred got on the bus and walked halfway down before finding an open seat next to a gentleman reading a book. He glanced at the title, *Destiny's Highway—The Beginnings*, and then stared ahead and brooded. How did his life get to this point? How could he salvage what was left of his business, not to mention his relationships with everyone in his life?

He thought about Pam and for the first time he felt guilt. He loved Rosa, but she was such a wreck and he was so tired of trying to carry her emotionally. What he got from Pam was the attention and support he wished Rosa could give him. If Rosa could provide that, he might be able to love her again and let go of Pam. It was up to Rosa to keep him from cheating and make him happy.

"Excuse me," the man next to him said.

Startled out of his thoughts, Fred looked at the man next to him. "Yes?" he said.

"I'm sorry for being nosy, but you look very sad. Is everything okay?"

A little irritated, Fred also found himself feeling a little better that someone cared enough to ask him how he was feeling. "No," he said, "everything is not okay. I mean, it's not awful, but, oh, hell—it *is* pretty awful," he said and chuckled a little ruefully. "But you don't need to hear about that. It's nothing I can't get under control with a little work. My name is Fred," he said and reached over for a handshake. "What's your name?"

"My name's Frank. I've had a rough go of it myself, so I recognize the signs."

"What's been going on with you? More importantly, how did you get past it?"

"It's rather a long story. Are you sure you want to hear it?"

"I definitely want to hear it. If nothing else, it'll help me forget about my own troubles," Fred said and chuckled.

"Okay," Frank said. "Sit back and get comfortable."

Chapter 15

Have you ever wondered how you got to where you are today? It's one of those questions that invariably a person asks and not surprisingly it always seems to be asked when the person is going through a tumultuous moment in their lives. When things are good and everything smells like a bunch of roses, the need to question the value of life isn't as pressing. It's only when life is looking at you from a dark cloud that the person asks what is the meaning and value of life. You ask this question because right at that point in time you wonder if it is all worth it. You wonder about the meaning and you look for purpose when there seems to be none. When I look back at my life I see a lonely little boy trying to survive and there is a part of me that actually feels a sense of relief that little guy is still around because I now realize that there are so many out there like that little boy that never made it.

My parents were typical hardworking migrant people. I was born in a communist country almost 40 years ago. My father came from a family that grew up in the Second World War and I would soon get to an age where my father would repeat stories of how tough it was during those times. Most times it revolved around how cold it was when it snowed, how many miles he had to walk to chop wood to keep the house warm, how long it would take to walk to school (more often than not in the snow), and how old he was when he got his first pair of shoes. My father was a proud man to say the least.

My mother on the other hand was a person of great sympathy. She was and is a person of great humility who could express emotion. In many ways she was a simple person who was uncomplicated and simply did what needed to be done. She was a survivor. I think I inherited bits and pieces of both my parents as one does.

I have asked my parents what I was like when I was a kid before we left the old country and came here to Australia. They told me that as a child I would sit on a step by myself with my hands under my chin in deep thought. I think another way of putting it was that they thought that I was an old soul. I don't know what an old soul is meant to be, but when I asked my father for his definition of it he would simply say that I was a sentimental person. Kids are supposed to be free and easy. Or maybe this is just what society leads us to believe. How would you know? Now that I have become a parent with my own children, I can see that little kids have so much more depth to them than I ever thought possible. I think it takes living through something to realize what it all means. All in all, I was a soft-hearted child back home and what was about to happen when we came to Australia would challenge that.

We came to Australia amid a flurry of activity with government representatives here to meet us at the airport. It was a big deal back then for a communist country to send a government sponsored company to a Western destination for the purposes of conducting business. My father was a proud and educated man and the fact that he was in the position to be calling the shots for this company was something that gave him great personal satisfaction.

So here we were, fresh immigrants coming to a new land and not really knowing what to expect. As it turned out, we ended up settling down in a country town with a modest population of about 30,000 people. Country towns are unique. They are vastly different to their counterpart city slickers who are constantly on the go. Country folk do everything slowly. Whether it's drinking, eating, talking, or whatever—these places seem to run to a very slow beat. They are also unique for being very territorial and when a family of strangers comes into town, they notice it. And if this family happens to originate from another country, then this notice is amplified exponentially.

I learnt what it meant to be different at a very early age in my life. I had to learn the hard way. The first thing that springs to mind was the fact that I didn't know the language. Within a few months of landing in the country, I was going to school not knowing how to communicate with anyone. The following is going to sound strange. I can actually remember sitting in class as a new student back then, and I can actually envision the teacher talking to me in English, and yet I could not understand what she was saying. It's like I am being transported back to that first moment in class and just sitting there not understanding anything that is being said. It was an incredible introduction to my survival training because in the end that's what it became. It was about survival for me and it's something that I have honestly carried through my entire life. I was an incredibly soft-hearted kid and that softness was soon tested.

People have this picture of children being carefree and totally liberated. There's no doubt that the aspect of innocence or how it is perceived by adults gives rise to the idea that kids are stress and worry free. I think this is way off the mark. I believe a lot of these misconceptions are driven by the adult having a reference point where the immediacy of life's pressures of today is a stark removal of the lack of such pressure when they were much younger. It has to be expected that kids and how they view the world has to be more carefree given that more often than not they have a parent who does the work and takes care of them. Kids don't have these particular worries, but other things occupy their mind. This I learnt very early on.

As a kid one of the first things that I struggled with was friendships—I had none. Yes, I played with other kids, but this was very temporary and fleeting and reflected the desire for instant fun which would be quickly followed by isolation. To put it simply, other kids played with me, but they got to the point where they would walk away from me when all the play was done.

I have plenty of memories of my childhood when we came to Australia. When you look back at those years and recall certain events, you have to wonder what it is about them that stand out over others. For me, if I were to be honest, then I would have to say that those moments were with sadness or some element of disappointment. I don't want this to come across as if my childhood was filled completely with misery and suffering because that's not the case. There are millions of people around the world who know what real suffering is and I certainly was not exposed to that. But my moments affected me in their own way nonetheless.

Growing up it soon became obvious to me that I was different. It's funny when you hear people say that because aren't we all different? I think that the real value to this lies in the sense that the people around treat you as if you stand out separate from them. I didn't fit into the group and because of this my interpretation was that I was different. People judge you in a certain way and your reaction to this judgment is to believe it and take it on as if it really represents you. If people around you tell you that you are an idiot and they say it enough times, then eventually you believe you're an idiot. When you feel like this, the only thing that you want is to be accepted.

This is an important point because the guy that helped me who wrote these *Destiny's Highway* books embraces this very theme of understanding something through knowing what its opposite is. I wanted acceptance and I knew what acceptance was because I wasn't being accepted. I knew I was different because my name was different than everyone else's. I wanted to be a Smith, rather than have my odd-looking and odd-sounding surname. It didn't help that my surname started with a letter near the end of the alphabet and was the last name called in the class. When it came to roll call, I waited for what seemed to be an eternity for my name to be called and when my name was finally called, there would be snickers and whispers.

I think that dealing with things became the motto for my life. At every step of the way I had to learn how to deal with what was thrown at me. If it wasn't the name calling, then it was the language barrier. And once I conquered the language barrier, I could then understand the hurtful things that were being said. Isn't that strange? You know you want to be able to understand the language so you can communicate with people, but when you do you realize what people actually think about you. That typified many outcomes for me. If I wanted something and it happened I soon wished I hadn't wanted it in the first place.

Primary school became the arena that would determine who I would become. I was a pretty conscientious student which reflected more the fact that I had few friends and really just saw the schoolwork as a way of having a break from the kids around me. Along the way it soon became obvious to me that my parents and in particular my father thought very highly of education. Even at that young age I began to feel the pressure of wanting to do well in order to make my father proud. I loved my dad back then and I still do. I don't blame him in any way for this as I guess he was simply doing what any parent does and that is to motivate his children to become something by getting a good education. That meant doing what was required of you in class as well as doing your homework.

I became a child that was always on edge and I believe that this was fundamentally associated with the environment that I was in. Michael has a term for this and that is Marine/Soldier. Everyone knows what a soldier is—a person that goes off to war to fight. But there is more to a soldier than simply fighting. How do soldiers deal with tragedy and horror? How do they deal with the constant threat of death? They learn to cope or more precisely survival kicks in and the soldier starts to cope with this constant pressure by learning to switch off. They become cold to everything around them as they deal with their feelings. This is the point.

It's not the situation that is the issue but the feeling that comes with it. So the threat of war on the outside is overtaken by the war that has started on the inside. And that war is a war with one's own feelings. You don't realize just how powerful your feelings are. People assume that logic is enough of a safety switch to prevent the person from doing things drastic, but all too often we see people doing things in response to their feelings whilst the logical mind has been well and truly taken over. Feelings are so incredibly powerful.

This is the whole point to this is that it's about you looking at you. So as a kid I became a soldier of education in my attempt to deal with the lack of acceptance from the kids around me and wanting to impress my dad. The more I focused on schoolwork the better I became and the better I became the happier I became. So I looked to school for happiness.

Being the studious person that I was, I made the decision to take an entrance exam for a private school which was the only one located in the town. It was a fairly prestigious school in terms of its position, so getting to go there would have been a big feather in my cap. I was in my final year of primary school at the tender age of 12 and I committed myself with the support of my parents that I would undertake the exam and if I was lucky enough to get a scholarship, then I would go to the school.

As it turned out, the only way that I was going to get in was the scholarship program as my parents were process workers in a factory. There was just no way that they could afford the full fees. I was acutely aware of this and set out to do my best. I just wanted to do my dad proud. I knew how much he valued education and I guess I did too, despite my young age.

Well, I went to the exam and feeling all the pressure around me, I succeeded in getting the scholarship. I think it's safe to say that it was about this age where you are no longer a child, but you aren't a grown up with an adult mind either.

When it came to enrolling, I could see the sacrifices that my parents needed to make just to pay for my school uniform to go to this school. It honestly beats me up inside thinking about this. I was by far the poorest kid in that school compared to everyone else. Every other kid there came from wealthy families whilst we lived in a housing commission estate and my parents worked as process workers in the local factory.

I turned up to school knowing that I had to perform to do justice to the fees that my parents were paying, not realizing that at that age I already had a stomach ulcer inside me. My stomach was always in pain and I ended up going to the doctor. He decided I needed to have an x-ray for a more comprehensive analysis.

When it came back, my parents were in shock and I guess I didn't really understand the implications of this condition. They put me on all of this medication and to this day my stomach has always been weak. I don't think I ever recovered from that.

That was the least of my problems though. Whilst I could hide the fact that I had an ulcer from everyone, I couldn't hide the fact that my breath smelt badly right throughout high school. It was terribly embarrassing. I was a very shy boy as a result of this and the fact that I already felt like a stranger due to lack of trust with the local people resulted in me gravitating to the kids who came from overseas because they were outsiders and since I was one myself, well, you know what they say—birds of a feather flock together. For the first time in my life I felt like I had friends. The Asian kids took me under their wing and despite my oral dilemmas they gave me credence as a human being. My affinity with these kids and their region of origin is something that I have held onto all my life.

Whatever problems I had in primary school only got worse in high school. If I felt embarrassed about my name before, then now I would feel ashamed every time it was called out. Whilst other kids got driven to school in expensive vehicles, I rode my push bike regardless of the weather conditions. I never talked about my parents because that would mean revealing to people their employment situation.

So it continued on. I went through high school and never had a girlfriend. I never kissed a girl or did anything with a girl. I never had a friend in high school that was a local kid. All my friends were foreigners. All of the above became constants in my life for that entire period.

One situation that still haunts me to this day was a school excursion to, of all places, the local factory where my parents worked. I felt shattered at the prospect of seeing them there. And the fact that I felt this way filled me with shame and still does to this day. I contemplated being absent for the day, but I resolved to go there and just hoped that I would be lucky enough to not see them. When you feel like this, it fills you with anxiety. The sense of embarrassment that I had was equally matched by the sense of shame that I felt. Here I was trying to avoid seeing my family, the same family that supported me and gave me the opportunity to go to this school.

Sure enough from a distance I could see my mother toiling away. At that point I could have shrunk into a shell and disappeared. My mother turned around and saw me and I quickly turned my head and pretended that I didn't see her. I felt gutted. After nearly 25 years it burns me inside at what I was doing.

Back then I was fighting back the tears which I always seemed to manage to be able to do. Someone once told me that your feelings can travel faster than anything in the universe. If something happened to you in your distant past, then the recollection of that moment hits you like a flash years later. You can get transported back to that moment as if it was happening right here and now.

And this is what I am feeling right now. This was one of many moments when something like this would happen. I went into a shop once and tried stealing a naughty magazine only to get caught and luckily the shopkeeper showed mercy on me and let me go. I jumped on my push bike and cycled away as fast as I could, pissing myself from the fear of the moment and vowed to never go back into any shop for fear of doing something stupid like that. Another time my sister and I nearly burned our house down and I ended up waiting in my bedroom for my dad to come back, feeling this dread and fear at what would happen as a result of my actions. And another time I got bitten by the next door neighbor's dog and ended up going to hospital to get stitches and then spent years being petrified of dogs. It goes on and on.

The common denominator is fear. It has always been such a dominant part of my life. If things went sour, then my reaction to that event was expressed through fear. I felt cursed by it. It hung over me and I always felt it was something that I was going to die with. I would have dreams as a child where I would get into fights and I would just freeze in the dream. Even in my dreams I couldn't conquer the fear. It was in my dreams that the core to my character would get revealed.

Many people remember some television show from childhood that had an impact upon them. In my case it was Dr. Who and my memory of this show was all about fear. If I went back into my childhood then there is no doubt that my earliest palpable sense of fear was expressed watching this show; that's how profound it was. It affected me so much that I have no doubts in saying that it contributed greatly in bringing out this debilitating feeling. Okay, sure I got teased and I didn't know the language and I had no friends and all that stuff, but in reality they weren't what I would interpret as moments that brought out fear in my life.

Dr. Who, on the other hand, was a television show that was science based and invariably had characters that consisted of robots as characters that scared me greatly. The robots that really got to me were called the Daleks. These robots looked plain evil to me, but what got me was their trademark remark, "Exterminate, exterminate," that would haunt me.

And haunt me it did. It's fair to say that this show only potentiated the effect that the other things were having in my life. I became extremely nervous and anxious watching this show and afterward I found it difficult to not think about it. But I was a glutton for punishment because the very next day I would be in front of the TV waiting to watch the show again no matter how badly I felt. It was almost like I had to prove to myself that I could watch it without feeling the way that I was, but this became terribly self-defeating because the end result was always the same. I would simply feel petrified and the constant thinking about the show afterwards only served to heighten my problem.

Fear works in different ways with each person. In my case, one of the most profound effects that it had on me was that it ruined my confidence. I was already a kid that suffered terribly from a lack of personal belief for reasons already explained, but if watching Dr. Who did anything, then the effect was twofold. First, it introduced fear into my life and kept it there hours later. Second and most profoundly, I became a young boy that didn't believe in myself. I had so much in the way of doubt about what I could face even at that age that everything after that seemed to follow or got worse as a result of this.

It's amazing how something like this could have such an effect, but on the rare occasion when I've discussed what I went through with my father years later, his comment would revolve around mentioning how I was sick and he would refer to how badly I reacted to that television show.

It occurred to me that I developed a stutter at the same time that I started watching this show. That was something that I had simply forgotten amongst all the other things that seemed to dominate my life. But in this moment of quiet solitude and reflection, I retrieved another memory that included my nervous speech, otherwise known as stuttering. It was something that I hid from others around me at school but not from my parents because I could easily go to school and not talk to people. That was a given. When you don't have much in the way of friends, then keeping quiet and to yourself isn't that hard. However when I got home I would have to talk to my parents and they started to notice my stuttering. All this from a television show that I remember to this day.

To try and overcome the constant fear which others sensed and subsequently used against me with me becoming a target, I decided to take up martial arts as a way of dealing with it. I got into it with a passion, and with my all or nothing obsessive attitude I would train first thing in the morning and at night by myself along with the formal training with my teacher. This became my place to escape and an opportunity for me to become the person that I wanted to be but was not.

Martial arts became my salvation. It was something I would use to forget how I truly felt about myself. And if it gave me the opportunity to defend myself, then that was a bonus. It introduced me to a spiritual element that I knew was there but was never answered by conventional thinking in the West.

Once I realized the Eastern way of thinking, I became hooked. It was a matter of engaging in a lifelong search to better yourself on a spiritual level. Even back then I knew that on this level I was broken. It's hard to not see yourself any other way given my fear of a television character, my subsequent development of what so called professionals would label as childhood obsessive compulsive disorder, my stomach ulcer, my bad breath, my lack of friends, the constant name calling, and anything else that I may have forgotten. How do you honestly feel good about yourself when these things dominate your life? I mean you can't just hide from it.

My father looked back upon those moments, especially when I had the Dr. Who issue and the OCD and would comment by saying that I was "sick." He had no other way of dealing with it other than saying that. He felt that I was sick in the head. At the time it crushed me that he thought that, but I knew he wasn't being nasty. Some might think that I am making excuses for him, but I have reached closure on this topic by coming to the realization that my dad didn't know any other way to deal with all of this. How would I feel if I were him?

At some point you have to find forgiveness for those people that have hurt you—whether it was intentional or not—or it will ruin your life. I was hurt on a daily level by so many kids who would refer to me with abusive labels, but I forgive them all because I know that they were too young to know any better. It's called empathy. Sometimes you have to step outside yourself no matter how hard this may be and see things from their perspective without judgment. Ultimately, I didn't want to do to them what they did to me. It hurt me a lot, but retaliating with vengeance solves very little.

When I first started going out with my girlfriend 18 years ago, I wondered what she saw in me. There would be many times during the course of my relationship where I would question the value of me as a person and why someone else would want to commit to me. Many years would pass before I would be able to look in the mirror and acknowledge that it was okay for a girl, any girl, to be with me. At any time I expected her to want to just break the relationship off.

This is not to say that I lived in fear either that the

relationship would end as I think it was something I guess that I simply pre-empted. I don't want to be critical of my wife back then, but there would be many times where my wife would threaten to break up with me. It would be a shock at first and if I wasn't already anxious in disposition, then I soon would be. I could never understand how she could be so volatile. I was so caught up in my own world and how I felt I suppose I didn't give consideration to how other people happened to react.

Being in a relationship is challenging in many ways. You put so much on the line and invariably with love comes sadness. The capacity to love and its recognition comes from knowing sadness. They are both part of the same coin and yearning for one brings on the other. I got to know and learn about love and in the end found myself experiencing a fair amount of anxiety along the way.

I didn't stay with my wife because I felt I couldn't get any better. I knew all too well that going through life thinking that the next girl will give you no grief is unrealistic. It's not so much that she gives you grief; both parties are as guilty as the other when it comes to this. The more I got to know my wife the more I realized that she had a story to her life and sadly it was one that was filled with much angst.

When you get to know someone after a while, it becomes obvious that once the facade melts away there are aspects to the person's character which may have seemed confusing before, but now things are a lot clearer. Her early childhood was filled with a lot of happy moments, but sadly that would be overtaken by a marriage breakup and the separation of her mother and father and the animosity that accompanied it had huge repercussions on the whole family. A once tight family bond that disintegrates leaves its mark on everyone and it's also something that becomes generational. Once a person gets scarred it's very easy for them to pass this on to their children who then pass on to their own kids whatever they experienced. I never understood this myself, but I soon became witness to its effects in my own relationship.

Our relationship progressed as all couples do and we eventually got married. Whilst it is fair to say that there were times when it was turbulent, I would suggest that it had its ups and downs like any marriage. It certainly was comfortable enough for us to want to have a child and luckily enough for us my wife had no problems at all in getting pregnant. Once the baby was born, we found ourselves with a beautiful baby boy who showed me something about life that I was not aware of prior to becoming a parent. When you partner someone and love develops, you become exposed to a type of feeling that with it opens up many doors to your personality.

How selfish are you? How strong is your ego? How angry can you get? These are the questions that get asked and invariably get answered when one falls in love. However when you have a child, things move to another level. The love for a child is something truly unique and quite different to the love expressed in a relationship with your partner. I truly believe that once you have a child your understanding of love taps into another part of your soul. I don't wish to be patronizing or degrading to people out there who have never become parents. Some people do it out of choice whilst others intentionally choose not to have kids for their own personal reasons and that's fair enough. Ultimately, if you have never had a child you won't know what you are missing out on.

I thought I struggled with self-confidence until I became a parent. If I questioned my value as a boyfriend or husband then I really struggled after becoming a father. I guess there is no easy way of saying it, but I thought I wasn't good enough. I immediately felt the pressure of knowing that it was my responsibility to be the principal financial provider for the family and I wondered if I had the mettle to be able to achieve. I was worried about my employment situation despite the fact that my job was secure. We had a two-door car and I could see that people around us questioned why the car wasn't bigger. Meanwhile, I would think about all those people in the poorer countries who had no car or any transport for that matter, yet here I was surrounded by people who couldn't get past the fact that we had a small car.

As a man you get left out. If your wife happens to breastfeed, the baby cries, and even when you pick it up it will keep crying until you hand the baby over to the mother for a feed. I felt like I was nothing more than the person that did this, and if I wasn't doing this I was changing dirty diapers and invariably handing the baby over to my wife again as the baby was always looking for a feed. Every man understands this, but it doesn't stop you from feeling left out and at times feeling like shit. In my case I started feeling like shit a lot.

The fact that my sleeping patterns changed started to take its toll on me. The days of me sleeping through the night seemed finished forever and I honestly did myself no favors at all by going to bed late to accommodate my tai chi training which I would do late at night as well as get up early in the morning to do the training again and then go to work.

I had spent many years training in the internal martial arts with a teacher that would soon become an ultra-huge part of it and his confidence started to wear off onto me but in a way that I didn't realize at the time was quite negative in the end. I felt quite invincible in some respects and, as such, thought I could burn the candle at both ends without consequences. I had done this for many years and thought I could continue with this practice, but that would soon reach a climactic point.

My diet was poor at the time, and whilst I would hardly engage in take-away food, my vegetarian lifestyle coupled with drinking copious amounts of strong green tea to the tune of three to four litres a day is what sustained me. There were many times when I would wake up totally exhausted from minimal and always broken sleep. I would find myself sleeping on the train trying to catch up on what I had missed out on during the night. When the best part of your sleep takes place on a train, you have to start questioning whether or not it's time for a change. In my case I think it only gave me false confidence that I could keep sustaining this practice. The mindset that I had was that if I could survive up until now then surely I could keep going on.

Things between my wife and I were at times strained. My wife, like any new mother, struggled with her lack of sleep and the constant demands of the baby. So while I struggled with not getting attention from our child, she struggled with the fact that the baby constantly wanted her and given the fact that I could not offer a breastfeeding alternative, the pressure really was on her.

On one particular day we happened to have an argument that quickly degenerated into a heated exchange, at which point she made a comment that she would be leaving along with the child. For many years I had been exposed to her reacting like this before we had children, but now the threat to leave with my son shook me to my core. I left the house and ended up going to a park just around the corner from our place to get my head together and it was here that I started to feel really anxious. The more I thought about it the more anxious I became and with my mind racing, I started to feel overwhelmed by my thoughts, which would be quickly accompanied by the terrible feeling of panic.

This panicky feeling was something that I had experienced many times as a child, but this time around I really found it difficult to deal with. For a brief moment the thought of losing my child represented a great loss to me. I felt like I had failed terribly as a husband as well as a father, whilst I imagined myself being one of those unfortunate parents who had occasional access to his child. I didn't know it at the time, but this moment in the park following the threat from my wife was the start of something. This would signal my slide downwards and I had little knowledge of just how things were going to develop. It would be brutal and there would be daily moments when I would feel like I was in the fight of my life.

Regardless of what other people around you may think, if it feels that way for you, then the thoughts and feelings truly do become real.

Before I became a parent I had visions of me never smacking my children, never giving my kids a pacifier, never feeding them fast food, never giving them chocolate, and whatever else a parent that wants to be perfect sees themselves doing. On all counts I failed. And with each failure I would question my capacity as a parent. It is fair to say that I felt like a failure. Both my wife and I struggled from the moment we bought our baby boy home. No matter what we did we could never seem to get the boy to sleep properly and for the first 17 days I slept in a separate bedroom in the hope that it would assist my wife deal with his atrocious sleeping patterns.

It didn't work. I really thought that by sleeping in another room that this would give my son a quiet place in our bedroom to sleep better. But this was just my way of introducing control that was never going to work. I didn't realize then, but the more you try to control a situation like this, the more disappointed and disillusioned you become. This was a perfect expression of a feature to my character that contributed to my anxiety—trying to control things that could never be controlled. I would learn this the hard way.

As time went by I became more and more anxious. It started to put a lot of pressure on my marriage because I was so wound up and given the pressure of being young parents, there are times when you just want to have some time out, but I just couldn't do that. If we went out to the shopping center, I would constantly worry about losing my kids to the point where I would simply not be able to take my eyes off them for fear that something would happen. If I picked up my child to hold him in my arms I would imagine him falling out of my hands and landing on the floor. I would especially become paranoid about this to the extent that I started to avoid holding him as it would just make me feel uncomfortable.

If I went to work and it had been raining on that day,

then I would be constantly worrying about my wife having an accident with the kids in the car. I would have dreams about this. If we went out with friends to take the kids to the park, the other parents could easily switch off and turn their backs on their kids whilst they played, but I would have to keep a constant eye on my own children. This would happen on so many occasions that after a while the other parents would look at me and I could sense that they could see that I was in a panicky state.

My wife would get terribly upset with me during these moments, as it would bring the attention onto us as a family unit with the possibility of a negative judgment from others. I would like to say that I didn't care about this attention, but in reality I wanted to be them. I wanted to be the parent that could just kick back and let my kids be kids, but that wasn't the case. I would feel guilty at this overt negativity and I would often lie in bed at night and hope that my growing darkness wasn't going to have an impact upon my kids. It saddens me to say this, but I can't help and think that it did. Maybe this is me being overly harsh with myself, but I have to be honest and accept that children do pick up on their parents' negativity.

When kids don't sleep, then it's fair to say that the parents will struggle to sleep as well. I was one of those parents that could hear my kids cry at night. And they cried every night. We weren't blessed with children that would go down at night and sleep through the night. I would get jealous and angry listening to other parents tell stories of how easily their own kids would go to bed and then fall asleep straight away, whilst our first born would wake up two, three, or more times a night. It was exhausting.

You don't always realize how much of an effect that lack of sleep can have on a human body, but after this experience I can see why sleep deprivation is used as a form of torture. In my case it was self-inflicted as well. I can't just blame my child's sleeping patterns solely on my lack of sleep. I was terribly obsessed with my tai chi training in my pursuit for perfection and I would train from the moment I woke up until I went to work and then finish the night off before I went to bed with another training session that would last quite often past midnight. If you factor getting woken up during the night a couple of times and then waking up at 5:00 in the morning and doing this every day, then you start to get a picture of what I was putting my body through. My wife would constantly get on my case about it, but in typical fashion I would ignore her at my own peril. How did I survive with so little sleep? Well, during the week I would catch a train to work which would last approximately 90 minutes each way and this is where I would get my best quality of uninterrupted sleep during the day. It was nothing for me to sleep the entire trip and I would often find myself in a complete sleep daze whilst walking the last ten minutes to work. As I said, I was exhausted. But this didn't deter me and the combination of drinking up to four litres of green tea a day to keep me going only fueled my bad habit.

How long can you keep sleeping four hours a night of broken sleep? How long can you rely upon getting your best possible sleep on a train to work each morning? How long can you keep drinking litres of tea each day to get you through, convincing yourself that your diet is good enough when in actual fact it is not? How long can you maintain an anxious disposition in all facets of your life before things just boil over? How long?

I went to work one day after a short night yet again of broken sleep and found myself in the company of others feeling like I was in a daze from sheer tiredness. I can recall now looking at a particular person and for some unknown recess in my mind I had this thought that I was going to yell an obscenity at this person in front of all these people. This immediate thought shocked me and in a flash I found myself staring at the person frozen in fear at the prospect of doing this.

And with that I could feel this incredible wave of fear soar through my body as my heart started to pound. I knew where the exit was and I had this overwhelming fear of needing to run out of there and just get to safety, or what I perceived to be safety, anyhow. I didn't yell any profanities and I didn't run out of the room, but that was the moment when things changed for me in my life.

At the conclusion of this gathering my mind raced at a million miles an hour as I thought about what had happened. I felt this immediate need to go back in that room and prove to myself that I could be in the company of others and know in my heart that I was not going to do what that thought which came out of nowhere suggested.

I didn't realize it at the time, but this was just the start of the treadmill that you get on when the driving force is fear. For the rest of the day I felt blown away by it all. There was no way that I could discuss with my colleagues what had happened for fear of being judged a lunatic. I just kept quiet about the whole thing and hoped it would go away.

Judgment is terribly cruel when it's directed by others, but when it's the judgment you hold within yourself, then it's the very worst of any kind. There is nothing worse than being critical of yourself, because the criticism never stops. It can't. How can it when you're doing it to yourself? How do you forget about something like this? As much as I wanted to go to bed that night and hope that I would wake up the next morning and all would be forgotten, I discovered that that was never going to happen.

Leaving work that afternoon, I walked to the station and jumped on the train and for once I didn't get any sleep. In the past I would simply jump on and sleep for the journey, but that day I sat on the train and felt anxious for the entire journey. All I could do was think about what had happened earlier. In my heart I just wanted to tell someone in the hope that they would at least tell me that I was not going crazy and that I had simply had a one-off experience of uncontrollable panic. Looking around on the train, I realized there was no one and the more I looked around, the more conscious I felt of the growing anxiety within me.

What is anxiety? If you researched it, you would find that it's a whole host of symptoms that encompass feelings of heart racing, shortness of breath, sweaty palms, and overall large secretion of sweat all over the body, a sense of losing it in the mind with the over-riding feeling that you are about to go crazy, and the list goes on.

My anxiety was totally centered on the feeling that I was going to go crazy. It was as simple as that. The sense of dread and overwhelming feeling of catastrophe has to be felt in order to be understood. It is hard to describe, but you feel like you're treading water and holding on for grim life with the sense that sooner or later you're going to stop and then die. It's that powerful.

From the moment I had that experience, it was only a few hours later when I found myself on my regular train trip waiting to go crazy before complete strangers and getting shipped off to the loony clinic only to lose my kids and my wife and the life that I had come to know. It was horrendous. By the time I got home, my wife could sense that there was something wrong. I tried to ignore her efforts to dig down to the source of the problem as being at home in the presence of my kids and my wife simply brought on shame. Before that moment I had felt intense anxiety—getting home I felt ashamed and embarrassed.

Furthermore, I couldn't help feeling that dread, as it brought home a feeling that I had tucked away nicely 30 years ago in the hope that it would never surface. But that was me lying to myself for all those years. That was me thinking that I could get away with sweeping things under the rug unresolved. The dread that I felt on that day as an adult was the same dread that I had come to know as a young boy going through all those moments of childhood angst that pressed down on me to the point where I felt totally out of control.

Michael G. Quirk

Control—or lack of it—is a strange bedfellow. To a large degree we live our lives living in denial, and then we reach an age where we know death is waiting for us. We also know that that the moment we take our final breath is a date that could be in the next moment or years from now. None of us knows, and as such we walk through life pretending that everything is cool until the moment comes when we can no longer deny that it is staring at us in the face.

The very next day the pressure valve could no longer hold back the emotion. I got up and jumped on the train like I normally do to go to work and I just sat there. I tried to ignore the previous day and what had happened, but I couldn't. The butterflies sat in the pit of my stomach and swirled around like a cyclone. Try as I may, I couldn't get it to stop. And that's what I was trying to do.

When I think about it now, I realize just how futile this was. Unless you've experienced anxiety like this, it's almost impossible to imagine just how you feel. I have often thought about the best way to describe it and I've come to the conclusion that no matter what metaphors you use, it still falls way short of the actual experience.

I have read extensively on this subject. I've come across recommendations incorporating love, darkness, forgiveness, acceptance, letting go—whatever. It's presented to you in such a way that you wonder if they're talking about an internal switch that you hit and miraculously things change in an instant. But it's never like that. That switch doesn't exist and if it does for those people writing on the topic then kudos to them because I've never found it myself, try as I might.

That day on the train the only thing that was immediate to me that I could do was focus on my breathing. I had this sense of anxiety that manifested itself the form of fear that I'll never forget. I sat there and looked around at everyone on the train just wondering if they knew how I felt. I wondered if they thought I was crazy because that's how I truly felt. The butterflies in my stomach were so intense that they started to overwhelm me to the point that I almost felt immobilized by them. I was on such high alert that I could feel my inner self buzzing from the electricity that was the fear coursing through my body.

I felt craziness. It was the type of craziness where you think that at any minute you're going to collapse onto the floor of that train and just writhe around in an uncontrollable manner demonstrating just how much you have lost it. I waited for it to happen. I could feel the judgment from my fellow travelers and I thought about my wife having to visit me in a mental institution with my children, which would have been my crowning moment to confirm just how bad the anxiety was. It never happened.

At that point I never thought of that. It didn't occur to me at the time that the fact that it didn't happen was a good indication that it would never happen. Instead I just played the waiting game to descend into sheer craziness. That was my ultimate fear. It brought back memories of how as I child I would go and play soccer on these grounds which were situated right smack bang in the heart of a mental institution and I would even at that age be fearful of these people that stayed in these places as they walked around in big groups. Other kids would gawk at them and perhaps even tease them whilst I would just stand back and fear the sight of them. They represented what I didn't want to happen to me and given the emotional dramas that I had already come to face, I was acutely aware of the fine line that exists between where I was and where they were. Or so I thought. The truth of the matter is that the only thing that I knew was what I was going through and although that distance between them and me may have seemed narrow the reality is that I really had no idea what it meant to be them. This is a truth for all of us.

That train trip was one that I would never forget for many reasons. It opened up the flood gates to what would truly be a life-changing moment. My life would never be the same and three years on from that moment I can wholeheartedly say that the person I am today is very different to the person that I was before. I have forgotten who that person was. This desire to be the person that I was is something that would over a period of time crush my will. It really did.

I arrived at work and all I could focus on were the butterflies in my stomach. I was worried that people around me would know what I was going through, which made me feel increasingly uncomfortable and only increased my anxiety. I kept waiting for disaster to occur. Although it didn't, this did nothing to show to me that I was in the clear; rather it heightened the sense of impending disaster. I think when you expect something bad to happen and you feel it in your core, it's almost impossible to deviate from this path. Because of that, all you do is wait. It's like you're willing it to happen in an almost obsessive manner.

I left work to catch the train home and it symbolized the point I had come to. I just kept focusing on my breathing and wishing that the panicky thoughts would go, but they didn't. I got home and I felt relief walking through the door as it signified a place of safety I could retreat to. However this would be short lived.

When you experience anxiety your mind races at a million miles an hour. It feels like it is beyond your control. You have thoughts popping into your head from everywhere and for me this is when it became overwhelming as if I was living a nightmare. They were brutal. It shook me to my core. It was like a door had opened and let out all the things that scared me the most.

That night I couldn't get near my kids or my wife without having a thought that involved them being harmed in some way by me. I had flashes of thoughts of me wreaking harm to them and that crucified me. I knew that none of these thoughts were true and I knew that I would never do any of these things to the people that I loved the most, but the fact that they were there in my head gave me incredible anxiety.

I processed these thoughts over and over again in my

head like I was trying to prove to myself that I was not capable of committing these acts. It's hard to explain, but I was visualizing the thought that would result in me panicking, and then continue this process over and over again. It didn't stop. That night as I lay in bed, I cycled through my mind all these thoughts. My very last thought before I hoped to fall asleep was that I would wake up the next morning and things would be different.

Luckily that night I fell asleep. I think I was so mentally exhausted from the day's events that my body yearned to go to sleep. The very next day I woke up and as I lay there I could feel the events of yesterday creep up on me. In the space of a few minutes I was throbbing in anxiety. I didn't know what to do. I had no choice but to lie there in bed and as it was still early I hoped that I would fall asleep again, which I did.

I woke up some time again and the butterflies were there. I could describe what I went through on that next day and the days after, but I'll get to the essence of what I was going through. I knew after what I had experienced as a child that I had what is referred to as obsessive compulsive disorder or OCD. It didn't take long for me to do what everyone else does these days and research this condition on the Internet. What I read on the computer fit me to a tee. I read it again and again after that on numerous occasions trying to convince myself that this is what I had and that I wasn't going totally crazy. It's terribly difficult to assure someone in that mindset that things aren't worse than what they were before. For me, the next step was going to be a huge challenge and it was something that I had to work up the courage to do, because it involved my wife.

After a few weeks of going through this, I felt an incredible loneliness at not being able to speak to someone about what was happening to me. It hung over me and became a cross that I had to bear on a daily basis. I guess I was looking for relief by being able to talk to someone, anyone. But who could I do this with? There was absolutely no one out there that I felt like I could trust or confide in. The shame and guilt along with the resultant judgment that I was sure would be directed at me was overwhelming. I felt that if I said anything to anyone, then my kids would be taken off me.

I came to the conclusion that no matter how much I would have insisted that these intrusive thoughts were not something I could ever do, I felt that no would believe me. So how do you go about dealing with this, especially when there is a part of you that needs to be able to talk to someone about this and not be judged?

I made the decision one night when my wife went out that I would copy the contents of the information onto a file and then print it out for her to read. This is another example of me avoiding things. There was no way I could sit face to face with my wife and come clean on exactly what thoughts were racing through my head. I just couldn't do it.

When I look back upon this moment. I can see that the need to approach my wife in this way outweighed giving consideration to the possibility of staying quiet on the subject and waiting to see a professional. I mapped out in my head all the different ways that my wife would react and with this I came up with a suitable way, or so I thought, of dealing with whatever way she reacted. As they say, even the best laid plans come unstuck.

I sat my wife down and confessed to her what I had been going through without getting into the specifics. I then gave her the document and asked that she read it carefully. After she read the first page I could see that she was starting to get upset and it wasn't long before she had to stop reading it because it was clearly affecting her too much. Seeing how she reacted was one of the most brutal moments that I have faced in my life. I had no control over the situation and I just waited for her to tell me that she could not trust me with the kids, which would have broken my heart.

That didn't happen, but I knew from that moment on that things would never be the same with us again. It got to the point where I started to explain to her what OCD was. I will explain OCD in a simple way. For me there is no point presenting an overcomplicated explanation because really it's unnecessary. It involves having what they call unwanted or intrusive thoughts which mean exactly what they suggest. The reaction to this is degrees of anxiety. Some people obsess so much about these thoughts that they'll compulsively act out rituals like switching a light on and or off or washing their hands repeatedly or counting in a particular way in order to alleviate the build-up of anxiety. Other people don't have these rituals and instead will deal with these thoughts on a mind level. The thoughts and anxiety go hand-in-hand and the process repeats indefinitely. The sufferer feels like a prisoner inside their own head and it puts them on constant edge with no sense of relief.

For me, a typical day was like the following. Each morning I would wake up and instead of lying in bed enjoying the process of waking up slowly, I would feel compelled to get up immediately. Lying in the darkness, staring at the ceiling whilst the anxiety started to throb through my body wasn't exactly the best way to start the day. I would do tai chi for about 30 minutes and that for me was like heaven; it truly was. It was my singular moment where I would be able to quite literally switch off my mind, go through the form and forget about the fact that during that period I actually felt normal. I have no idea what my life would have been like without it.

It got to the point that doing this training was my major escape and I have to say that there were many moments when towards the end of the practice I would start to experience anxiety. This baffled me because it felt like what I was doing was self-defeating since the whole point of the tai chi was to at least alleviate some of the symptoms of the anxiety. What I didn't realize was the fact that I had developed such an attachment to it, that my knowing that it was coming to an end meant that I would have to open my eyes and face the world. This was avoidance on my part and I was in that much denial I didn't recognize it.

After this I would quickly guzzle down my breakfast and then face my nemesis, which was the train journey. This is when things would heat up. The whole trip was a nerve-wracking experience where I would be self-conscious about the people around me and whether or not they knew I was projecting anxiety. I would have thoughts rush through my mind where I anticipated a panic attack, or I would have the thought that I would jump off, or that I would crumble onto the floor. I'd think of any catastrophe and I owned it during these trips.

By the time I got off the train I would be a bundle of nerves and I now had to walk the remaining 10 minutes to work. I had to walk over a bridge and every time I imagined jumping off. With each traffic light I came to, I would stop to watch the traffic go by and I would imagine stepping in front of a car.

There was no respite when I got to work as I would have to deal with the intrusive thinking of saying something to my work colleagues or I'd have the thought of hitting them or that some disaster would happen. It was not uncommon for the butterflies in my stomach to be so bad that I would be glued to my seat. When I finished work, the same traffic lights would wait for me as would the train journey. By the time I got home I would be in such a nervous state that I'd do my tai chi training—ignoring my family—just to settle my nerves. My training was my only moment of peace. As much as it meant to me, it also took me away from my family, but I just had to do it to not feel everything else.

That was my day. The weekends were not much better and the fact that I had more free time since I wasn't committed to work only facilitated greater nervous thinking. Try as I may, I could not escape. I had to do something and the next step was to see someone; I made the decision to see a professional.

Destiny's Highway

I knew that I had OCD and I knew that I had bad anxiety, but something in me wanted me to see a psychologist so they could either confirm my self-diagnosis—or confirm that I really was crazy. Fortunately, they confirmed what I already knew and this gave me immediate relief.

I think that's all I really wanted—to hear from someone else that I wasn't crazy. However this relief was short lived. I had arranged for follow-up sessions, but in the meantime I did what everyone else does and researched my condition via the Internet. I became obsessive in this regard and it didn't take long for me to become an expert on not only my condition but a whole host of other serious mental health disorders of which I was convinced I had. When you couple that with the fact that my employment meant that I worked on the front line with people who actually had these serious mental health disorders, it's easy to see how I couldn't hide from my fear of going crazy with these conditions. It was unavoidable and at times felt like I was being punished.

Over the next couple of weeks I went to work carrying this new, professionally-confirmed label of myself. It started to grate on my mind that I now had a disorder. No matter what I did, I now felt a strong personal identification with it and I saw myself not as the person that I always had been, but a person who had been pigeon-holed by a profession of individuals who wore white coats and pretended to know who I was and the journey I had been on. But that wasn't the case.

They didn't know me and their understanding of what I had remains problematic to this day, and that's being kind to them. Putting that all to one side, I started feeling like I was carrying a cross that quickly became too heavy for me to carry. It was one more thing that added to my anxiety. It's easy to do research and read, and people tell you that you should avoid coffee and get regular sleep and abstain from watching television shows that create tension and anxiety. But the fact is that it's all unrealistic.

Michael G. Quirk

I live in a world where I'm compelled to get up and go to work. My work entails me to come face to face with people who have at times committed serious and heinous crimes. These are people who demonstrate severe mental disorders, so I had no chance whatsoever to avoid this because I faced it daily. Did it exacerbate my anxiety and soon to arrive panic attacks? Yep, it sure did. I could go to bed earlier to get extra sleep, but I still woke up to two screaming kids who needed to have their diapers changed and that resulted in broken sleep yet again.

Sooner or late you have to face your demons. You just can't leave society and then come back when you think you are better and assume that you'll now be able to deal with the heat in the kitchen. The point is to find a way of dealing with this heat whilst it's in your face. It's a cruel and harsh way of looking at things but it is the truth.

So off I went to my second visit to the professional and by the end I had been armed with breathing techniques I could practice alone. So that's what I did. The very next day I focused on one element of this where I would consciously focus on listening to sounds in the room with my eyes closed whilst taking long deep breaths. This then led to me giving attention to the sounds outside the room and finally I concentrated on the sounds outside all of this. Sounds easy, but by the end of this I was in a panic as I found myself becoming sensitive to the tiniest of sounds which resulted in me now worrying that maybe I was hearing whispers to these sounds.

This is the problem with anxiety. You are on such high alert that everything is accentuated as you are in that fight/flight mode. It is something that you have to experience to fully appreciate and from that moment onwards I became ultra-sensitive to the faintest of sounds. This was coupled with my fear that these sounds were whispers which would further confirm my fear that I was hearing things which would have further cemented an even greater fear that I now had a serious mental illness like schizophrenia.

Fear creates more fear that builds even more fear, so I then started researching schizophrenia. No matter how many times I read it, I couldn't convince myself that it was a condition that I didn't have. I had even confessed this to the psychologist who went out of her way to tell me that I didn't have it, but sadly I couldn't be convinced. If it wasn't schizophrenia, then it was bipolar; if it wasn't either of them, then it was something else. So on and on it went. I set about crucifying myself at every available opportunity and there was no stopping the intrusive thoughts that served as fuel for the anxiety. After two visits to the psychologist I found myself feeling even worse than before.

I decided to go to another consultation, but in all honesty I think I had made the decision to end the sessions. All I wanted was to get better, but this wasn't happening. The type of therapy used was called cognitive behavior therapy. I don't want to be critical of it, but I really think in my opinion that it misses out on some key elements. Let me explain.

When things started to peak and I quite literally began unravelling, as I've said, I did what most people do and that is consult with Dr. Google. There was such a pressing need for me on a feeling level to scour the resources of the Internet so it could somehow tell me then and there that I was not going mad. So I started researching. The more I researched the more I kept checking different resources just to keep convincing myself that what I was experiencing was a type of anxiety commonly referred to as OCD. However I was never satisfied with the diagnoses offered on these sites and so, as I said I felt compelled to see a trained professional with the view to have them tell me that I had anxiety and thus prove to me that I was not going crazy. So off I went to see a trained psychologist who ultimately told me after the first consult that I did in fact have OCD, which is a type of anxiety. Now here is the thing. Did I walk away from this diagnosis and feel relieved within myself that I had just been told by a professional that I had a type of condition which was something other than being told that I was going crackers? Well, yeah, it was a relief. However a strange thing happened after that. In the weeks leading up to my next visit I started taking on board the diagnosis to the extent that I became a slave to the label! I now referred to myself in the following way—"I am Frank and I have OCD". I was now no longer Frank but Frank with a disorder, and that's the key. When you meet with these professionals you walk away with a disorder. You are broken. There is something wrong with you. You are not the same as everyone else. Do you start to get the picture? How can you feel good about yourself when you have an expert confirm that you are broken? There is just no way around this and it weighed heavily on me. I tried to rub it out of my memory by ignoring it, but in the end I may as well have been trying to erase a tattoo. It was there to stay. Here is the irony. I was so desperate to see someone so I would not feel crazy, but in the end I was given a judgment by that person which I then started to use against myself! Can you believe it? Well, when I got to the second consult after having to wait a few weeks since the first one I got introduced to Cognitive Behaviour Therapy, or CBT. Essentially speaking it is collaboration between the therapist and patient where the patient is taught to recognise unhelpful thoughts and emotions and learn to deal with them by relearning with different strategies. It sounds all good, but what I have learned now is that it misses out on some key points. More than anything it does not acknowledge the role that thoughts and feelings perform. It pretends to but fails. It fails because it requires an intellectual type judgment when recognizing what is viewed as negative type thoughts, but in reality what it is essentially doing is using the same mind to try and fix the problem through logic. There is no acceptance, and those that argue that there is, can't escape the reality that *you* have labelled the thought as being either positive or negative. Now it's all plain sailing when the thoughts are great, but when they are negative then we have a different outcome. You are not taught to feel.

You are not taught to let the feeling wash through you. You are not taught to let the feeling do whatever it needs to do and ultimately you treat feelings as an enemy to avoid when things are really down. But how do you pull yourself out of the darkness when you are in the darkness? You just can't with CBT. That's why people get stuck. They don't know how to deal with the feeling in the first place. They aren't taught that the feeling is there to tell them what they aren't doing for themselves where it counts and that is on the inside. That's the problem. CBT works from a base of dealing with the negative. If you label it as negative then it will always be that way no matter what technique you employ. But if you are shown that *all* your feelings and thoughts are there to awaken you then things become different. It's only when you are stuck in complete darkness that you become aware of just how powerful a little light is. And you can only see the light in the darkness. But no one wants to embrace the darkness!

So anyhow, back to my story .At this point in time, where it became obvious to me that for all the reading and researching I had done, very little of this had helped me. In fact, I had become worse and started to experience panic attacks. I was lucky to not deal with them on a daily basis, but they were brutal when they did occur.

To this day I have memories of three of them which left an indelible impression on me. The first one took place one morning when my wife had gone to work and I was left with my son, who was in the kitchen at the time. He simply sat on the kitchen bench looking at me with his beautiful innocent eyes and right next to him were our kitchen knives sitting neatly in a holder. At that instant I became aware of them and with my son sitting there right next to them I had this intrusive thought that I would pick the knives up to hurt him with. As quickly as this thought invaded, I had this incredible surge of adrenalin race through my body as I experienced my first true panic attack.

Of course I never did anything to my son, but this

moment permanently scarred me. For the rest of the day I replayed that scene in my head over and over again trying to convince myself that I was not capable of doing something like that. The fact that I had not done anything was lost on me. The shame that I felt at just having that thought was brutal. This summed up what I went through. All it took was a single thought to ruin my day. That day disappeared, but the thought stayed with me. That moment defined what I went through daily.

I once read about a female nurse who had OCD who found out that one of her patients had committed suicide. She then found herself in a frenzy thinking that she would do that to herself. I went into a frenzy obsessing over whether I would do that to myself as well; that's how easy it was to send me into a spin.

The second panic attack took place one morning when my son came into bed with me and my wife. I lay there awake to the situation and was basically staring at the walls hoping that I would go back to sleep. I don't know why, but things started to change all of a sudden and I felt this incredible surge of panic grip me. I could sense that my son was next to me and it was almost like I felt like I was failing him or about to fail him and I froze. I literally could not move, and knowing this only exacerbated the situation. I felt an incredible wave of energy that was nothing more than horrific fear that came and went in what felt like an instant. What happened after that is a source of amazement to me that remains like that to this day.

Within half a minute I got up, unlike the frozen state that I had been in only seconds prior, and went outside to perform my daily ritual of doing my Tai Chi. It blew me away doing this! I thought about this for the whole day and I have to say that I reasoned that I somehow needed to have that panic attack to release the buildup of anxiety. Go figure.

The third panic attack was by far the most severe. I was on my way to work I had decided to occupy my train trips by engaging in some reading of spiritual books that I hoped would somehow change my life. On that particular day I happened to be reading Eckhart Tolle's *The Power of Now*. I was trying to put into practice the principles of being a witness to my own mind which is something that I had been trying for about a month, but was failing miserably.

The end result of this practice was that by trying to be the observer, I felt like I was watching a horror show play out in my mind which made me even more nervous. I don't want to be critical of Mr. Tolle on this, but I have to say that it's very easy to promote the concept that one should make acceptance the backbone to everything that one does, but it's not so easy to actually make it happen. Acceptance was something that was very foreign to me. Words mean very little. What counts is making things happen in a very real way that reflects on an internal level.

I got off the train and started walking the rest of the way. I walked past the bridge and once again the intrusive thought of jumping off entered my mind for what seemed the millionth time and this is where things started to go bad. I looked into the distance and I could see a work site. I kept my focus on what was in front of me and it was here that my sense of movement went haywire.

I don't know why, but I had this sense that I wasn't getting closer to what was in front of me, but I knew that was walking. I started to panic because the two seemed incompatible. The more I looked, the more it seemed I was not moving, yet I knew I was moving. Bang! I had the most horrendous panic attack, and it flooded me with so much adrenaline that I couldn't feel my feet.

Feeling this only intensified the moment, and all I could do was try and focus on my breathing. It did not relent and I was just willing it to go way which only made it worse and it was here that I started to lean to one side as I knew the fear was that bad that I was about to faint! I don't know how or why I didn't collapse, but I came out of it only to find myself just shaking uncontrollably inside. I stood at the set of traffic lights at the bottom of the hill where I usually had the invasive thought that I would jump out into the traffic only this time around no thought entered my head as the shaking was just too strong. It overpowered everything for that moment. Nice way to start the work day.

This is what my life had become. I had incredible panic attacks combined with minor ones. I sensed anxiety inside me that seemed to drown me. The only free moment I had from the anxiety was when I did my Tai Chi or when I went to sleep at night. I was totally besieged by unwanted intrusive thoughts to the point where I started to feel like not going home at night so I didn't have to hug my kids and have an unwanted thought about them at the same time. I didn't want to engage in any sexual activity with my wife because the sense of arousal seemed identical to the feeling of anxiety, and that was something I wanted to avoid at all costs.

I felt like the worst parent and, in fact, the worst person in the world. Such was my shame. There wasn't a single person in the world who I truly felt I could talk to about what I was going through. I hoped and hoped that I would go to bed at night and fall asleep and wake up the next day a different person, yet it never happened. I yearned to be the person that I was before all this started, but then I got to the point where I forgot who that person was. This was my life.

One day I picked up the telephone directory and started to ring around in search of a therapist who might help me. I had no expectations of this person and I think that by simply looking for someone—anyone—that it gave me the faintest hope. That's what my life had become. It had got to the point where the mere act of looking for someone gave me breathing space, and I guess showed me that I was willing to keep up the fight.

I called some numbers and spoke to a few people who seemed professional enough but lacked real sympathy in their voices. I finally spoke to someone who was different than all the other people I had spoken to and decided to make an appointment to see this guy.

His name was Michael and it's fair to say that this is where my new journey began. When I first went to see Michael I was desperate. I was a broken person who had long given up the hope of going to bed at night and waking up the next day feeling like a different person. I felt like a prisoner—and I was.

Jail isn't just a place where they close the door and lock the key. It is also the place that resides in your head and when you look at the world, crippled by the way you feel and think, only then do you realize just how precious it is to wake up and feel normal. You lose sight of what normal even is. All you know is that you don't want to feel the way you do.

I had tried everything, and I mean everything, outside of going to the chemist and taking medication to stop the anxiety. When you feel like you no longer have any choices left in your life, then you have to question what life is about. Everything that I thought I knew no longer had the meaning that it once had. I had valued education and work and trying to make some money to provide for myself and my family. I had placed value on having children and getting the house and paying that house off as soon as possible so we no longer had debt. I wanted to be something in the eyes of my kids.

I realized that none of those things matter. They're all man-made societal constructs and it's very easy to get caught up in all of these things, but they mean absolutely nothing and have no value whatsoever when the proverbial shit hits the fan. You can have all of those things and more, but when you feel like I did, then you can't enjoy any of them. Not in any way. In fact all of those things that you put value on only serve to bring you down even further because of the lack of completion that you think will give you some sense of accomplishment. You realize that it doesn't work.

With Michael I felt like I could talk and not be judged. The reason why that was the case was because he understood what it meant to have empathy. To understand something truly is to demonstrate it fully in your behavior.

On the very first appointment I found myself crying uncontrollably within ten minutes of sitting down, after having touched upon the subject of my father. I hadn't expressed emotion like that in years. When people talk about bottling up emotion, what they mean by this is releasing it. It's funny, isn't it? I got a very early introduction into understanding certain concepts, not by the concept itself, but by its opposite. You only know what it is like to bottle up your emotions the very moment you finding yourself releasing them beyond your control. That moment of emotion was the first of many moments like that.

We are brought up in a society that, at the end of the day, is a man-made construct. We're indoctrinated very early on through the mechanism of fear that we have it forced upon us rather than having the opportunity to embrace it. Parents teach their children through fear. Don't touch the fire because it will burn you. Don't play near strangers because they might snatch you. Don't eat that food in case it gets stuck in your throat and you stop breathing.

We don't teach our kids, but rather instill fear along the way and think that we are tutoring them in growing up. We lie as parents. We teach our kids that there is a Santa Claus and a Tooth Fairy and an Easter Bunny when we know that none of these characters are true. It's a lie and the society that we live in is based on many lies. It's lies that keep the economic machine going because we have to convince people that they it's all good to work your guts out and then get married, followed by the kids, which is followed by the house, which comes with the debt that lasts forever, and this is all supposed to be happiness.

But it's not. I judged myself. Every day that I got up to face that crippling anxiety and thinking that I was going crazy was me judging myself. You judging yourself is the cruelest judgment of all because you can't run away from it.

I could no longer try to keep running away from my feelings. It just wasn't working. Not that it ever does. I barely got through the day given how terrible the anxiety pressed upon what seemed every nerve in my body. I looked forward to going to sleep just to have a break from it. I was mentally exhausted from it all. I was like one of those mice on a running wheel going nowhere.

Along the way I had read spiritual books on loving myself and acceptance, but what I learned here is that there is no magical switch to hit and all of a sudden the love starts to pour in. All those self-help gurus wrote about something that sounded good on paper, but in reality they delivered something that I felt I was trying to achieve, but couldn't. You see, this is the point. If you have to try to be happy, then this can never be true and everlasting happiness. The key to changing my life lay in empathy.

To explain what empathy is, I have to take you on a small journey.

Each time I went and saw Michael he would describe empathy in a different way in the hope that I would somehow get it. At first I struggled with this. It had nothing to do with Michael, but with the fact that I was in a place where I couldn't see the light of day. I was the proverbial dog under the house that had hidden from the world and didn't want to come out.

What you don't realize is that you do all of this to yourself. It's not the people around you that are judging you that counts, but rather the judgment that you give yourself. I struggled on a second-by-second basis with the sort of thoughts that I was having, to the point where I would hang out to see Michael and tell him in great detail about all of them in the hope that he would look at me and say it was all cool and that I wasn't going crazy.

You see that's the thing. I didn't understand why I was having them at first and it never occurred to me where Michael was in his understanding—but this would change. I soon discovered that Michael really didn't place emphasis on the type of thoughts that were taking place. That meant nothing to him. What mattered was the feeling behind them and this led to one of the most brilliant insights—feelings run the show.

What do you do when you are so down you are stuck in a bedroom all day long, day after day after day, unable to move? What do you do when you have to get up each day to go to work and you have a train journey waiting for you that fills you with anxiety from the moment you board until the moment you get off?

What do you do when you go to the kitchen and you see the knife set in front of you whilst your kids are nearby and you get flooded by thoughts that you might hurt them even though you know in your heart you never would, but the mere fact that these thoughts are there sends you spiraling?

What do you do when you jump into your car to drive to work and every time you see a person walking along the road a thought jumps into your head that you will run them over?

What do you do when the anxiety hits you so hard that every cell in your body feels like it's on high alert to the extent that the smallest of sounds become thunder to your ears?

What do you do when you feel so ashamed inside yourself that you feel like crying, but you don't because you just keep doing what you have always done and that is block it away?

What do you do when you just want these thoughts and feelings to go away but they don't?

What do you do?

It's easy to read self-help books and it's easy to take fish oil and it's easy to go to bed early each night to get a good night's sleep and it's easy to practice deep breathing and it's easy to avoid things that elevate your stress—but at the end of the day what you really want to know is what do you do when the thoughts and feelings inside your head and heart are so intense that you feel absolutely terrified with fear, and the more you hope this goes away the more it doesn't, but gets worse?

Destiny's Highway

The first thing that you have to realize is that everything that you've been doing up until this point doesn't work. If it did, you wouldn't be feeling this way. You then realize that by doing this you've been using props that have become a part of your life. These props represent the way you deal with stuff. If you're exposed to judgment from an early age and you take this on board and then judge others, you don't realize, it but you are judging yourself. Without empathy you will look at that homeless person muttering to themselves and think that they are loony. Eventually that's what you will call yourself, and when that happens it is like nothing that you can imagine.

We go through our lives being taught to block our feelings. From a very early age it's impressed upon us that expressing emotion, especially if you're a man, is perceived as weak. You do everything that you can to avoid showing emotion and you have plenty of allies to assist you in doing this—drugs, work, sex, sports, medication, and alcohol—all of these serve to cover up what we feel.

In the end, all of this leads to avoidance. Unfortunately, you can't keep running forever. What ends up happening is that feelings always win out. You never realize that by blocking these feelings that you're doing something completely unnatural. If I asked you what sort of day you had, your answer would be about how you felt. What you know of the world comes from what you subjectively feel. When you feel calm, the world seems calm. When you feel like fainting from anxiety, then the world in front of you looks like it has the power to swallow you up. But nothing has changed. It's not the world outside you that has become scary; it's the world inside you that feels this way, and then gets projected onto the canvas that you see.

When we're young we're taught how to read and write, how to go to the toilet, how to speak to people, and how to avoid bad things. But no one teaches us how to deal with the thoughts and feelings inside. If anything, you're told to not express those things. Think about how many times in a moment of frustration your parents told you to not cry and became angry if you didn't stop so they wouldn't be embarrassed in public. Later in life, when something bad happens, you don't know how to deal with it emotionally.

You have a panic attack that is so bad that you automatically start worrying about the next one. You feel butterflies in your stomach that just don't go away. You can't breathe properly. Your chest hurts from your heart pounding. You feel like you're going crazy. You feel like the world is going to swallow you up. The fear is intense.

Who teaches you to deal with this? How is it that something as natural as your own feelings feel like such an enemy to you that people over the years have killed themselves just so they don't have to deal with it anymore? How sad. How terrible that a person that's given the gift to feel feels so persecuted by this that they end their lives. How did it go so wrong?

This is what I learnt with Michael. I asked and felt all of these questions.

You can't run away from your feelings or thoughts. They can either represent something that's filled with horror, or you can see them as a way of guiding you. As much as you engage in the process of avoidance, all that you end up doing is putting more and more pressure on the moment when the whole system boils over. Believe me—it does.

If you can't run away from them and all the different ways of avoiding them don't work then what does? Realizing that what you have been doing hasn't been working is the first step. As long as you think that you can lean on past methods, then this will always conclude with past results. Some people call that relapse. Realizing that you have contributed to all of this is the next step. If you're a victim, then what are you a victim of? If you go through your life thinking and feeling that outside forces are to blame, then you've handed the power to someone else. What this means is that you have rendered yourself totally powerless. You have the power.

If a "good" thought pops into your head, then you react by feeling good. But if a "bad" one pops in, then you react with chaos. In the end, you choose how you react.

You have the capacity to look at your thoughts and feelings. Everyone does. Everyone has that part of themselves that can silently watch the thoughts and feelings play out their game. It's at this point that people tell you that you need to accept what is going on, but this is useless because you would've already done it if it was that simple.

This is where empathy starts. This is where you realize that how you react is something that you've carried all your life. I learnt that by going in and being a silent witness to what was going on inside my head took me back to how I reacted as a child. I acknowledged that. This is how my props were born. There was no need for me to continuously go back because that wasn't living, just a never-ending journey backward. I went back and I saw a scared little boy. Every time I got scared in the present it was no different to that scared little boy crying out to be heard. The answer was to go to that little boy and hug him. In other words, go to the most vicious thoughts in my head and hug them.

Why? Because acceptance means holding onto something first before you let go. If you want to be a person of courage, then you need to be put in a position where courage shines through. If you want to be calm, then you need to be put in a place where you can't avoid anger. If you want real happiness, then you need to hold the sadness. It's only when you're touched by the sadness that you go through to the happiness.

The more I consciously resented those thoughts and feelings and having to deal with the train and walking into the kitchen with the knives staring at me and standing at the corner with traffic going by and not being able to look at my kids because I felt so ashamed—the more it showed me how I wasn't able to be empathetic.

Real empathy is seeing that homeless bum muttering to

himself and smelling in the worst possible way and going up to that person and hugging them with love. It's because you don't want to do that to your own feelings, that gives your feelings their power. It's because you don't want to go there, that you at your core are scared. In the end, it's precisely that which keeps coming at you.

At the moment of intense fear, you have the choice to keep fighting or let these thoughts and feelings wash through you. Let them because they want to and they will keep knocking on your door unless you let them in. Breathe through them. Watch them do their best. Go for the ride with them. Encourage them even more and just when you think you're about to go completely mad from them, bring empathy in. Empathy doesn't judge. It's not the world that thinks you're going mad; it's you judging you.

It's time to hug you in exactly the same way that you would hug someone else who needed to be hugged to stay alive. It's you hugging you without judgment and without thought. That is the only real answer.

Chapter 16

Frank finished his story and after a long pause, he said, "Well, I guess I went on a bit, didn't I? My stop is coming up and I'm looking forward to seeing my son. I hope this helps in some way. Thanks for listening."

He then reached into his pocket and pulled out his card and handed it to Fred.

"Here is my number. If you want to talk again, please give me a call."

Frank got off the bus and left Fred sitting in a daze. At the next stop, Fred also got off, although he didn't know exactly where he was. He knew he was a long way from home, but he needed the time to think, so he pointed himself in the right direction and started walking.

Where had things gone so wrong? Why had he thought he knew everything when all along he was more messed up than he knew? He wasn't in control at all; it was all illusion.

He walked and walked and more and more he realized what a complete fool he had been. Why did he think he could find happiness by having an affair with Pam? Worse, all he was doing was hurting everyone involved—Pam, Rosa, and especially himself. What a miserable illusion that one was.

Then he thought about his children and he started to cry. He had been a horrible father and he knew it. He could never get back the years of their lives that he had wasted. Deb and Brad deserved so much better.

The more he walked, the more miserable he felt. He felt completely useless. His whole life had been a joke and the last few years were the worst. He had blamed everyone else for his problems, but all along it had been him causing problems for everyone else. His family would be better off without him.

Fred lost track of time and forgot where he was until he saw a school in front of him, the school that Deb and Brad attended. With a start he realized that tonight was the night of Brad's performance. He had promised he'd be there. Was he too late? Was he too late for everything?

By the time Fred walked in, the presentation was in its final stages. He stood at the back of the hall when the emcee made an announcement.

"Ladies and gentleman, students and distinguished guests. I'd like to introduce one of our leading music students, Brad Murray, who will perform a golden oldie for the parents and then one of his original compositions. Please welcome Brad Murray."

It seemed that Brad already had a fan base in the school, because as he walked onto the stage the applause was widespread. Deb looked around to see if her father had arrived. She whispered to Rosa, "Dad's here."

Rosa whispered back, "This is going to be interesting."

"Thank you. This song is one our parents might remember. It's called, "The Logical Song," by Supertramp."

> When I was young, it seemed that life was so wonderful,
> A miracle, oh it was beautiful, magical.
> And all the birds in the trees, well they'd be singing so happily,
> Joyfully, playfully watching me.
> But then they sent me away to teach me how to be sensible,
>   logical, responsible, practical.
> And they showed me a world where I could be so dependable,
> Clinical, intellectual, cynical.

Destiny's Highway

There are times when all the world's asleep,
The questions run too deep
For such a simple man.
Won't you please, please tell me what we've learned?
I know it sounds absurd
But please tell me who I am.

Now watch what you say or they'll be calling you a radical,
Liberal, fanatical, criminal.
Won't you sign up your name; we'd like to feel you're
Acceptable, respectable, presentable, a vegetable!

At night, when all the world's asleep
The questions run so deep
For such a simple man
Won't you please, please tell me what we've learned?
I know it sounds absurd
But please tell me who I am.

There was thunderous applause. People looked at Fred as if to say, "That's your son, isn't it? Aren't you proud?" Fred was dumbstruck. He was enraged and yet another part was proud.

"For my next song I'll be doing one that I wrote. I'd like you to welcome a friend of mine to the stage to help me sing it. Please welcome Lyn Booker."

Rosa and Deb looked at each other. "I didn't know!" said Deb to her mother.

Lyn walked out on stage to the applause. She and Brad stood together at the microphone. They smiled at each other. Lyn announced the song.

"It's called The Bird of Love."

When the morning dew is warmed by the sun
The petals from a rose begin to open,
As the sun warms the petals,
The perfume begins to rise

Michael G. Quirk

Then Brad sang.

As the perfume rises the air becomes filled.
Then as a bird takes flight it soars
It soars high above.
Soaring in the perfumed air

Then they both sang the chorus twice.

Love must be like a bird
Love must be like a bird
Flying in perfumed air
Neither held nor hindered
But free

There was a standing ovation; people yelled out 'More! Do it again!'

The emcee called out, "Would you like to hear it again?"

"Yes!" was the roaring reply.

The emcee concluded the evening with "I'd like to thank everyone for coming tonight. Let's give it up for Brad and Lyn!"

So they sang it again and when it came to the chorus, Brad called out, "Sing it with us!" and they did.

Once again they brought the house down and Lyn embraced and kissed Brad in front of everyone. They were over the moon.

As Fred stood at the back of the hall, people were filing out past him and congratulating him on Brad's efforts. Fred was stunned—his feelings were like a washing machine. He didn't know what to think or feel, so he just played along with everyone's notion that he had something to do with Brad's performance. He must have, he told himself, after all he was his father.

As the crowd left the hall Fred honestly didn't know how to act towards his family. He moved away and stood outside waiting for them to leave the hall.

Brad and Lyn made their way to the rest of the family; people were still congratulating them on their performance. Eventually they walked outside and saw Fred standing under a tree.

"There's Dad over there," Deb said, pointing at her father.

Brad saw him and tried to read his reaction. He looked sad; he hadn't seen him like that before. Deb had gone over to him and stood beside him.

"Can you ask Brad if he would like to come home with me?" Fred asked Deb.

"Sure, Dad."

Returning to the family group, Deb relayed the message to Brad. Lyn said she would like to come with him, but Brad told her that he would see her later—he was expecting a showdown that would not be pretty for Lyn to see.

Brad slowly walked over towards his father and Fred turned and started walking towards home. Brad followed him. When Brad caught up with him, Fred turned and looked at Brad. Brad thought, *Here we go again. I'm really in for it now, but I don't care anymore.* Brad realized that he was not afraid as he normally would have been.

Fred said, "Brad, that was amazing. You were really good. Well done!"

Brad looked at his father. He didn't know what to say.

Fred kept going. "When I was your age and younger, I liked music—I still do—but my parents didn't let music into our house. Their religion forbids it. As you know, my father was a minister in the church, so he had to set an example. Tears welled up in Fred's eyes. "My father threatened me with a gun held at my head, and he told me, 'If I ever catch you playing or listening to music, I'll kill you!'" Holding back his tears, Fred continued.

"Now I vowed that if I had a son, I would never, never bring him up the way my old man brought me up." Fred was finding it hard to speak. "Now I realize I have—I've done exactly what I didn't want to do." Now crying full on, he said, "I'm truly sorry for the way I've treated you."

Brad was good with hugging and that's what he did with his dad. "That's okay, Dad. No damage done." His eyes filled with tears as well.

On the way home, Brad realized he once again had the dad who used to take him fishing—the one that used to play soccer with him together when he was younger. Fred told Brad that he would like to learn to play the guitar and asked whether Brad would teach him.

Brad thought it a bit strange, but agreed.

When they got to their place, Lyn was there ready to sing some more. The Murrays asked the Bookers around and they had a party with Brad and Lyn leading the singing. The children hadn't seen so much happiness in their house for a long time.

Sarah and James seemed so close. Rosa was looking at Sarah from across the room and she was glowing.

"I know what you mean by glowing when you told me about Sally," said Rosa to Sarah.

Sarah looked quizzically at Rosa.

"Now you're glowing, too."

"Thanks. We're sorting things out. We still have a way to go, but we're getting there," Sarah replied.

Fred went over to Rosa and put his arm around her. She felt the gentleness of the man she married.

"I'm sorry, love. I want things to change. Tomorrow I'll call someone that can help me." He reached into his pocket and pulled out Frank's card.

About the Author

Michael G. Quirk was born into a working class, Catholic family in Newcastle, Australia, and graduated with a degree in civil engineering. He left the engineering field after six years and became a house-husband. Thereafter, he became a clinical hypnotherapist and graduated with a psychology degree. He has been a therapist since 1982.

Quirk is developing a method he refers to as an "All Heavenly and All Earthly Good" approach to life and healing. He works on teaching people to care for themselves on a spiritual level that he calls "Destiny's Highway." It is an approach presented as education, rather than therapy.

He currently resides in Australia with his wife and is the father of five children.

Learn more by visiting Michael's website at:
www.destinyshighway.com

www.ingramcontent.com/pod-product-compliance
Lightning Source LLC
Chambersburg PA
CBHW052209090526
44584CB00017BA/2082